Dear Marie,
I wish you
well and a sp[...]
Recovery. [...] my p[...] with Jean

11-7-92

Colors

Multicultural Inspirations
for Growth and Recovery

Deborah Stein

DEACONESS PRESS

ISBN 0-925190-58-6
Library of Congress Catalog Card Number 92-072159

Printed in the United States of America
96 95 94 93 92   7 6 5 4 3 2 1

Cover designed by Donna Welton
Chapter symbols designed by Andrea Williams

Publisher's Note: Deaconess Press publishes books and pamphlets related to the subjects of physical health, mental health, and chemical dependency. *Colors* and other publications do not necessarily reflect the philosophy of Fairview Riverside or Fairview Deaconess, or their treatment programs.

Acknowledgments

Many people have contributed to this book, and I would like to offer my thanks to:

Sandra Benítez, for suggesting the concept of the chapter headings;

Kris Ellis, for assistance in writing and editing;

Leigh, for her contributions on pages 46, 93, 117, 159, 199;

Ursula McCrary, for pages 58, 73, 101, 118, 123, 137, 142, 149, 156, 188;

Walter D., for pages 28, 38, 120, 143, 145, 177, 192;

I also gratefully acknowledge:

Deaconess Press, for believing in this project;

the gentle suggestions of my editor, Jack Caravela;

the unconditional support and encouragement of family members and many friends;

the research assistance of friends and associates, too many to name;

my sponsor, Mary Thomes, for her guidance and words of insight;

Andrea Williams, for her artwork and design suggestions;

and BJL, for the books, and beyond.

Finally, to those who offered contributions which I may have accidentally omitted from this list: please know that you have my heartfelt appreciation.

A portion of the proceeds from the sale of this book will be given to cancer research, in memory of Mother, and to programs for the still-suffering addict and alcoholic.

Introduction

Living together is an art...
William Pickens, from an
address given on November 2, 1932

Who am I? What am I? These are questions we all face, whether we are recovering from drug and alcohol addiction, compulsive gambling, hurtful relationships, eating disorders, or even a demanding and stressful day. This book evolved from my own exploration of these questions and from thoughts shared by others who continue to explore and create their identities through recovery.

Colors reflects the inspirational sources I carry in my heart. The quotes come from writers, thinkers, artists, scientists, and even from anonymous graffiti. Like the meditations which accompany them, the quotes reflect the diversity of our world.

We are a population of diversity, and cannot ignore the social context of cultural diversity in recovery. We come from different races, from different ethnic, national, and cultural backgrounds. We are of varying ages, religions, economic classes, physical abilities, sexual orientations and lifestyles. Especially within the recovery community, where self-knowledge and self-acceptance is vital, diversity demands attention.

The meditations in *Colors* acknowledge our differences and our similarities. I believe that embracing both can offer us fulfillment as individuals and as healthy communities.

In writing this book, I have drawn on the cross-cultural influences which have guided my life as a descendent of people of mixed ethnic and cultural backgrounds. I have also drawn on a variety of spiritual beliefs that have formed my own foundation for living.

The seven sections of *Colors* reflect themes common to a variety of stories told in many cultures. I chose this structure because all cultures have stories passed down from generation to generation, and the stories, folklore, mythology and legends of a culture are the source of that culture's customs and rituals.

The stories of a culture can reveal its spiritual history. When we pass on stories from generation to generation, we pass on values and attitudes as well, and it is from this tradition that we as individuals find our source of identity.

The seven sections of *Colors* are: ***Water***, ***Earth***, ***Sun***, ***Moon***, ***Animals***, ***Dance*** and ***Fire***. While different cultures give these elements different symbolic meanings, I chose the following interpretations from a blend of sources because of their symbolic connections to recovery.

Water fertilizes, preserving people, animals and vegetation. In the stories of some cultures, water is a giver of life, the source of *creation.*

Earth is universal, offering *promise.* Some creation stories tell of all life springing from the earth.

Delivering light, heat, and *vitality,* the **Sun** brings forth crops. The daily journey of the sun across the sky, and the mystery of its rising and setting, evoked the sacred in many ancient peoples.

Moon, as it waxes and wanes, symbolizes *cycles* of life. The phases of the moon were the earliest measurement of time. The moon is also a source of light and illumination.

Animals are sources of *wisdom.* In the folklore of many cultures, animals are the principle characters, offering insight and guidance.

Dance affirms *life* and preserves the order of existence. Throughout the world, dance is used to celebrate crucial cycles of life and nature, such as birth, friendship, planting, harvesting, and death.

Fire is *renewal* and restoration. It is a purifying element, used in folklore for symbolic cleansing.

Each of the seven sections includes twenty-eight readings, representing the twenty-eight-day cycle of the moon.

Colors does not assign a day of the year to each reading. Rather, you are invited to open the book to any section and select an inspirational reading. It is my belief you will find a relevant affirmation.

I have learned during my own growth and recovery to trust random acts. I find that what comes to me is usually what I need to hear. Grounded in my belief that I am exactly where I need to be spiritually and emotionally, I work to accept the lessons and opportunities offered. Perhaps this will work for you, too.

It is my hope that *Colors* will support your journey of recovery as you affirm the cultural traditions which shape your identity. Our healing depends on an understanding and acceptance of who we are as individuals, and in accepting those who are different from us. As we put our recovery into the social context of our lives, we become leaders by example. Showing others that differences are valuable can help build a healthier world for all.

I invite you to imagine with me the day when we all welcome our variety and our distinctions. We will then truly be rejoicing in life and in our diversity.

—Deborah Stein

Index of Titles

Guide to Readings

Water

creation

Water

Identity

...call it our craziness
our wildness
call it our roots,
it is the light in us
it is the light of us
      —*Lucille Clifton, "Roots"*

My efforts to make a moral inventory of myself lead me on the way to self-acceptance. I define myself and my needs and my desires. I can be open to the perspectives of others, and let those viewpoints be theirs.

On this path, I can let my cultural identity radiate. I will treasure all parts of myself. I can choose to redefine some aspects of my ancestry and still respect my culture and its traditions.

creation

One for All

Injustice anywhere is a threat to justice every-where. We are caught in an inescapable network of mutuality, tied to a single garment of destiny.
    —*Martin Luther King,* "Letter from a Birmingham Jail"

I will try to stay out of living in isolation. My life is tied to people of my culture and commu-nity, my race, gender, and at times, economic class. But it does not stop there. I am tied to the rest of humanity, and an injustice directed at anyone affects me as well as the rest of the human race.

My accountability to humanity begins with responsibility to myself. As I integrate the parts of myself into a whole, I see my relationship to others more clearly. I am able to stand for justice for all people.

Water

Birthdays

My favorite thing is to go where I've never been.
—Diane Arbus

Each day is new, and I am renewed in its freshness. This is especially true on the day of my birth, a day of remembering when I was called into being. On my birthday I recall past memories, and in my mind I picture celebrations and friends from over the years.

My birthday is a special day to celebrate, for my Creator has given me life. Today is a day for reflection, a day to recall the memories stretching behind me. It is a time to see where I have come from, and to look where I am now.

creation

Freedom

We wish no evil, harm or hurt,
To those who kept us down so long;
We join with them in ways alert,
To guard good freedom's happy song.
        —Marcus Garvey, "Centenary's Day"

My freedom comes first from within me. Challenges in my life can enhance my expression of freedom. In remembering injustices in the history of my ancestors, or in my personal past, I will see the past as a lesson to be learned from.

I am free to move forward from my past, and I recognize that external freedom does not ensure emotional freedom.

Water

A Place for Me

I have a great belief in the fact that whenever there is chaos, it creates wonderful thinking. I consider chaos a gift.
— *Septima Poinsetta Clark*

It can be frightening when everything seems to be out of my control. In the past, I might have reacted to this fear by trying to deny it, or by going to great lengths to try controlling it. As I recover, I learn to know the difference between what I can control and what I want to let go of.

I have also learned that when I feel out of control, I can center and calm myself by remembering to trust that I am where I need to be. When I trust in this, I can look at periods of chaos as unleashed creativity working its way to the surface. Knowing I have made the best choices, I can let this energy take me into the unknown. It will be a fitting place for me.

creation

Web of the Universe

Just as a pebble of intention dropped into a still pond ripples out in every direction, so the appearance and phenomena of our lives and our world are ripples on the serene surface of the universal mind.
　　　　—*Dhyani Ywahoo*, Voices of Our Ancestors

　　I embrace my connection to the human race, to the natural world and the universe. The web that holds us together is delightful. I understand that by living in honesty and with integrity, I strengthen the web of humanity and all of life.

　　What threatens any part of the web threatens us all, and I know that our well being depends on the well being of all. As I respect all of life, those around me may learn respect. They, in turn, will teach others. Love grows, and the web is protected.

Water

Continuity

Just because everything is different doesn't mean everything has changed.
—Irene Peter

In my recovery, I am working to create my life. This creation, however, does not mean starting over from scratch. As I create my life, I build on the foundation of my history. It is up to me whether my story will provide a continuity that can keep me centered or whether it will be an energy drain.

Acknowledging my cultural traditions affirms my connection to others and gives me a framework for creating my life. Acknowledging mistakes made in the past allows me to make informed decisions in the present. Denying mistakes or trying to ignore them, however, can end up causing me more problems and draining my energy. My past is still with me. But how it affects me is up to me.

creation

Decisions

Remember this: Every decision you make stems from what you think you are, and represents the value that you put upon yourself.
      —*Foundation for Inner Peace*, A Course in Miracles

    Most of us make hundreds of decisions each day. Some of them may not seem so important—when to get up, what to wear, whether to drive or take the bus—while others are obviously more significant.

    How I decide to think, act and feel reflects my inner self. I can choose to relate to people in anger or in kindness. Whether big or small, every decision I make reflects who I am and what I value.

Cross the Threshold

May your moccasins cross the threshold of Truth, And may your trail lead into the beauty beyond.

—*Mary Summer Rain,* Spirit Song

To cross the threshold into recovery, I need to transform my identity. I give up the security of my comfort zone and step out over the edge. And in creating myself anew, I discover my limitations. I learn I cannot continue certain behaviors and beliefs and still expect to heal.

I choose to seek dreams laced with possibility. I acknowledge the immense effort it takes to cross into truth. Now, as I move along a trail of beauty I had not imagined before, I can see the value of my efforts. Knowing what it takes to cross into truth, I treasure my recovery even more.

Humanity

You must not lose faith in humanity. Humanity is an ocean; if a few drops of the ocean are dirty, the ocean does not become dirty.
—Mohandas Gandhi

There is a difference between blaming people and holding them accountable for their actions. I know that blaming everyone of a particular skin color, sexual preference, gender or economic class for the hurtful and destructive actions of individuals within that group merely keeps me stuck.

My recovery urges me to accept the intrinsic worth of humanity in all our diversity. When I separate the individual from the prejudice, I affirm my own self-respect, my values and my ideals. Today I will remember to accept people for who they are.

Water

Action

*You can focus on your obstacles, or you can go
on and decide what you do about it. To me, it
breaks down to that: you can do and not just be.*
—*Gloria Dean Randle Scott*

I choose recovery this day, aware that my
choices determine my direction. Decisions coming from my center determine the best course of
action for me when meeting an obstacle. I have
a choice of how to respond. If I concentrate on
an obstacle, rather than on my options in facing
it, I risk becoming immobilized by the situation.
The obstacle zaps my strength.

Instead, I can examine my options and make
decisions based on the full spectrum of choices
available to me. Rather than trying to remove or
go around the obstacle, it may be better for me
to change course completely. Whatever I do, it
will be an action based on my choice.

Delightfully Different

In everything, no matter what it may be, uniformity is undesirable. Leaving something incomplete makes it interesting, and gives one the feeling that there is room for growth.
— *Yoshida Kenko,* Essays in Idleness

Different perspectives, cultural traditions and spiritual beliefs can all be sources of inspiration. The human spirit is often dulled when given strict guidelines of acceptability. When encouraged and given room to grow, our creativity can astound and delight.

A shift in perspective may spark a breakthrough. Today I will appreciate the differences of those around me. Accepting them as they are, I will value them for who they are and for how they differ from me.

Water

Building

People say, "What is the sense of our small effort?" They cannot see that we must lay one brick at a time, take one step at a time.
    —*Dorothy Day,* Houseman's Peace Diary

Each step I take builds on those I took in my past and forms the foundation for steps I will take in the future. Healing takes time, as I spring into a new me.

When I get impatient with myself or with the rate of change in the world, I can stop and look back on past successes. I can acknowledge and congratulate myself for all I have accomplished. As I go through today, I will see the value of even my smallest action. Each step forms support for the next.

creation

Loyalty

The problem to be faced is: how to combine loyalty to one's own tradition with reverence for different traditions.
—*Abraham Heschel,* I Asked for Wonder

Loyalty to myself and to my beliefs is easier when my vision is clear. Commitment to myself helps me maintain balance, and self-love integrates my experiences with my heritage and my dreams. I know it is difficult to deny the part of me that is my culture.

I can choose how to incorporate cultural traditions in my life. I can respect the choices my ancestors made within the context of their lives. If I am faced with what first appears to be a conflict between my cultural traditions and those of others, I can look inward to determine what is the best for me within the context of my life. I choose the course which will reflect my dreams and ideals.

Water

Miracle Making

Nature has created us with the capacity to know God, to experience God, just as it has created us with the capacity to know speech. The experience of God, or in any case the possibility of experiencing God, is innate.
　—*Alice Walker,* You Can't Keep A Good Woman Down

My Creator constantly presents me with opportunities, and provides me with the strength and support to go after them. Giving up fear removes my blinders, so I can see miracles around me.

When I turn my problems over to our Creator, I am turning over the fear and anxiety that prevents me from seeing the best course of action. This is different from renouncing my responsibility for taking care of myself. Giving up fear makes room for creative action.

Love without Limitation

Moments of unconditional love allow us to touch the vastness and depth of human experience altogether.
—John Welwood, Journey of the Heart

When I am able to love unconditionally, I free up my energy and open my mind to the wonder of life. Rather than allowing a relationship to be limited by prejudice or short-sightedness, loving unconditionally lets me realize the full potential of living.

Loving unconditionally stretches my boundaries. My senses are sharpened, my creativity is triggered, and my assumptions are challenged. When I give love without limitations, I am giving the nourishment of life. When I am loved unconditionally, I flourish.

Water

Grieving

Besides integrity and creativity, trust in yourself is essential in the art of grieving well, just as it is in the art of living well.
—*Alla Renée Bozarth,* A Journey Through Grief

Grieving is a personal process. Writing, talking to my friends, creating my own rituals...these are just a few of the ways I can acknowledge my transitions. Grieving puts closure on my past and makes room for my future. Today I acknowledge the grief I still carry and recognize that acceptance of it is the first step to integrating past with present.

In my recovery, I have let go of behaviors and beliefs I've held dear for a long time. Destructive as some of these were, they were part of me, and I felt grief and fear in letting them go. However, grieving for their loss is not a contradiction to recovery. Rather, it is a necessary part of my healing—it is a validation of who I am.

19

Choose Your Response

Freedom is what you do with what's been done to you.
—Jean-Paul Sartre

I will remember that I have a choice of how I respond to my experiences and those of others, and of how I will incorporate them into my identity. I can cry about injustices, I can rage against racism and discrimination, but I remember that inner peace will lift me above grief and defeat.

I recognize that I am the sum of all my experiences, all of my feelings, and all of my choices. Recovery for me means that I can create who I want to be within the context of my life.

Water

Visions

May you always unfold
your night wings inside
And treasure the visions
of the dreamer.
          —Mary Summer Rain, Spirit Song

Dreams guide my spirit; daydreams and night dreams alike. When I feel bogged down in routine, I let my mind wander where it will. Sometimes I let my mind roam by watching birds congregate—not waiting for them to do anything in particular, but just observing them. Soon my mind is drifting on its own.

Sometimes during my daydreams I will find a path through a point I am stuck on, or come up with a solution to something that has been bothering me. Sometimes I come up with a new idea. My subconscious is the birthing ground for my creativity. My dreams are the translation.

Food for the Soul

Imagination is the beginning of creation.
—George Bernard Shaw

Before I can create the life I want, I must imagine it. And to keep my imagination alive and active, it needs to be cared for—nurtured and nourished from within and without—just like the rest of me. I can feed my imagination by listening to music, reading, and surrounding myself with beauty. A fresh flower offers a reminder of the natural order of life. Sleeping animals remind me of natural grace.

I can learn of other ways of being by conversing with people from other countries, or by reading about other cultures and traditions. In addition to stimulation, my imagination needs periods of reflection. By centering myself and opening my mind, I make room for my imagination to ramble. Unhindered, it weaves dreams and establishes guideposts for me to follow.

Water

Communication

*And while some angels have abandoned their
  wings,
my voice, not so much indigo, not so much new,
  is something different.
...And my wish, no longer suspended,
  finally comes home.*
        —Nellie Wong, "Voice"

My ability to communicate helps me step forward and create a way for myself. My voice is an important one, and worlds will open as I express myself. The suggestions of my program of recovery direct me to make amends with those I have harmed. Sometimes this involves speaking with them, or writing to them.

Communication means freedom from silence; by doing these things I am led from isolation. When I stand in the midst of injustice or inequities, silence and fear may appear. Each time I give voice to my thoughts, I affirm myself, and my recovery is strengthened.

Gifts

Music, art, and poetry: they stroll among surprises.
—*Arnold Stein*

To reaffirm my healing, I draw on the gifts of music, art and poetry. Each takes me above my singular perspective and connects me to the universe. They speak to me on an instinctual level, quieting my rational self and letting me absorb their texture.

They are a tapestry that weaves my experiences with those of my ancestors and those of the people who will come after me. Today I will nourish my soul through the essence of all cultural heritage—music, art and poetry.

Water

Time Out

How beautiful it is to do nothing, and then rest afterward.
    —Spanish proverb

Sometimes I need to turn off the world, to do nothing and give my spirit time to renew. I can stop and do nothing but be outside or on the couch. Sometimes I need to step away from my responsibilities, projects and to-do lists, and just take time out.

Cutting off external stimuli gives my mind a chance to sort through my concerns and clear out accumulated clutter. Doing nothing gives my body a chance to truly rest. Afterward, I will feel refreshed and ready to go. My creativity will be heightened and my energy strong.

creation

Inner Sculpting

I do believe that it is possible to create, even without ever writing a word or painting a picture, by simply molding one's inner life. And that too is a deed.
    —Etty Hillesum

Some sculptors describe their creation process as removing clay that is not part of the sculpture. My inner sculpting is similar. To help the essence of who I am emerge, I must let go of what no longer is part of me: old habits, destructive thoughts, perhaps even friends or family members who threaten my commitment to recovery.

What remains is the whole of me: my history without the judgment and guilt, my actions and experiences beheld in the context of my life, my dreams no longer hindered by self-doubt and criticism. My essence has always been there, but every now and then I need to make sure the layers of clay are removed.

26

Water

A Perfect Time

Ideas too sometimes fall from the tree before they are ripe.
—*Ludwig Wittgenstein*

As I learn to trust myself, I come to accept that changes come in their own time. Taking action is implicit in my recovery, but sometimes no matter how much I want something or try to make it happen, I come up against barriers. If it seems as though my efforts just do not work, I can stop and review. I can ask myself if I've given my best.

Have I done what needs to be done, or did I let something slide? Shall I examine my goal and think about whether it fits my value system? How has my goal affected the people I care about? After considering the answers, I can decide how to proceed.

creation

Belief

Creator! you who dwell at the ends of the earth unrivaled... Where are you? Up in the sky? Or down below? In clouds? In storms? Hear us, answer us, acknowledge us, give us perpetual life, hold us forever within your hand. Receive this offering wherever you are. Creator!
—*Inca Prayer*

When first trying to turn it over to my Higher Power, I felt as if my life were a tangle of yarn, with one strand stuck under another. People told me, "Try getting down on your knees." I didn't know what that could get me except sore knees, but I did it anyway.

Although I never consciously found out how to turn it over, I learned to do it anyway, and my life is better. Now I tell people, "You do not have to believe in those mighty muscles. Just do the exercise." As I create my own relationship with my Higher Power, I keep in mind that all means of worship and meditation are valid.

Water

Trusting Today

The supreme value is not the future but the present. The future is a deceitful time that always says to us, 'Not yet,' and thus denies us.
—*Octavio Paz*

Today is important, so I will take time for the moments of today. As I walk the paths of recovery, I can learn to trust the present, which means trusting myself and others. Although the future is unfamiliar, I can begin to feel safe in the presence of the unfamiliar.

What is unknown becomes an adventure, a challenge and an exploration. As I heal, I will let the Creator of Peace guide me into recovery, experiencing the present to its fullest, as it offers glimmers of hope in my search for trusted ground.

creation

Serenity

Just be calm, be brave and true...
—Marcus Garvey, "Keep Cool"

In my recovery I value my serenity, where I find a softness, a quietness that heals and connects me with my inner self and with others. Serenity for me means being willing to acknowledge any limits society may place on me while still being able to love myself and my community.

If I feel or see barriers that divide, I can use the courage I have from my serenity to identify and discuss these obstacles. I will remember to speak from my authentic self, which I have discovered in my serenity.

Earth

promise

Making Room in the Garden

We plant seeds that will flower as results in our lives, so best to remove the weeds of anger, avarice, envy, and doubt, that peace and abundance may manifest for all.
    —*Dorothy Day,* Houseman's Peace Diary

Bindweed is a vine that will overwhelm all in its path. Its pink and white flowers belie the threat of being smothered by its growth; it is deadly despite its beauty. Negative feelings left unattended can also be destructive, smothering hope and energy. When I acknowledge feelings of anger or envy, I can stop their growth.

Still, I may need to let these feelings remain alive for a while. **They are valid and they** are a part of me. I can choose to keep my feelings in perspective and prevent them from running rampant. My belief in the possibilities of life needs room to grow.

A Strong Foundation

A thought of faith once awakened is the foundation of the way forever.
—*Abbot Zenkei Shibayama,* A Flower Does Not Talk

Having accepted my worthiness, I can now trust that my choices are made from a solid foundation of love and goodness. This foundation supports me in every way. It shores me up when I am having doubts, and clears my path as I move forward.

My foundation is strong enough to carry me for a lifetime, and flexible enough to cushion occasional falls. Reminding myself of the strength of my foundation, today I will stand proud.

Mother Earth

Mother Earth! We honor you as we honor our mothers. We thank you for all the benefits that you have bestowed upon us. You have given us food and medicine. You have provided shelter. You have given us beauty to behold.
—Ojibway Invocation, translated by Ben Johnston, Ojibway Ceremonies

As I heal, knowing a sense of connection to nature can aid in my renewal. By honoring the earth that is the source of life for all, I honor the perfection of my life force.

The earth offers us sustenance, if we choose to accept it. The earth offers us wisdom, if we choose to listen to it. The earth is a reminder of the abundance of miracles around us, as our sense of beauty and of life's possibilities is formed. I will honor the earth as mother of us all.

Releasing Hurt

Hear me, you who have the power to make grow! Guide the people that may be as blossoms on your holy tree, and make it flourish deep in Mother Earth and make it full of leaves and singing birds.
—Sioux prayer

One way I can enhance my personal truth is to look to elements of nature and the universe for guidance in letting go of what needs to be gone from my life. Letting go is a way to allow personal growth. Letting go in my recovery can mean it is acceptable to leave pieces of my past, or to release parts of my family, my community, or my culture that are hurtful.

This release enhances my identity. As I explore my individuality, I also remain a valuable member of my culture, and a valuable part of our global community, the world in which we all live. I am free to choose what fits for me and leave the rest behind.

Earth

Growing Day by Day

As long as you live, keep learning how to live.
—Seneca

Recovery takes forever; there will always be more to learn. Still, my continuing search for new ways to live renews and strengthens my spirit as I explore the world more deeply. I will approach each day ready for the opportunity to learn.

Possibilities for growth abound in my life. There are endless possibilities for expressing my creativity, for enriching my relationships, and for improving the health of our community and of our environment.

Prayer and Meditation

It isn't until you come to a spiritual understanding of who you are—not necessarily a religious feeling, but deep down, the spirit within—that you can begin to take control.
—*Oprah Winfrey*

I have a choice about the life I want to lead, although I did not always think so. At times I may have felt a victim of life, of society and circumstances. A tool of recovery is to recognize that I can only control my own actions and attitudes, and no one else's.

I used to ask my Higher Power daily to change my life, and then I'd spend my days wondering, wishing and complaining about why situations were not changing. Then I learned that prayer and meditation are not things to only do beside my bed at night. My prayers and meditations make a difference when I keep them with me consistently.

Earth

Speak Up

Say not, 'I have found the truth,' but rather, 'I have found a truth.'
—*Kahlil Gibran,* The Prophet

It is important to speak the truth in all areas of my life. A positive way for me to reinforce the truth is to stand in front of the mirror and speak my truths out loud.

Sharing my opinions with groups of people, or speaking up at work or in my family or community, develops the habit of living the truth. Every act of truthfulness reinforces my ability to see truth.

Name the Pain

*Look into yourself...although it may cause pain.
Be courageous. Face your faults...and know
their names. Eradicate them.*
   —*Kristin Zambucka,* Keepers of the
Earth

When I feel depressed or sad, I try to name
the cause. If I can identify the source, I have a
choice in how I feel. I may realize that feelings
of sadness do not have anything to do with my
present actions. If the source of my sadness is
disappointment in myself, naming it helps me to
face the disappointment and move through it.

Perhaps I realize that it is the anniversary of
a loved one's death. I can choose to continue on
with my day while acknowledging my grief, or I
can choose to forego my usual schedule and do
something in honor of my loss and my loved one.
In giving myself a choice of actions, I see what I
can do to comfort myself.

Earth

Language

What a great language I have, it's a fine language we inherited from the fierce Conquistadors... They carried everything off and left us everything... They left us the words.
—Pablo Neruda

There is beauty in the sound and feel of language. Our languages represent lessons handed down to us, and I am proud of the traditions and language of my culture.

As I move further into recovery, however, I am open to new ways of communicating. In times past, I may have chosen silence during adversity, rather than risking openness. I can add the new language of recovery to my vocabulary for a positive tool of growth and sharing. Language and communication can guide me through times of adversity.

Dignity

Nobody can dub you with dignity. That's yours to claim.
        —*Odetta*

My dictionary defines dignity as "the quality or state of being worthy." No one can make me feel worthy. This gift comes only from my self, and only when I love myself for who I am today, not who I would be "if only." Out of the love and respect I feel for myself comes my ability to act with dignity. This is one way of showing respect for myself.

I can show my respect and compassion for others by treating them with dignity. Dignified actions can also be taken on behalf of the world, by treating our environment with dignity. I believe humanity and the Earth is worthy of honor and respect.

Clear Sight

*Not everything that is faced can be changed.
But nothing can be changed until it is faced.*
  —*James Baldwin*

I acknowledge time lost in blaming others, the time spent waiting for a better moment, and time spent in despair. Accepting the past, I forgive myself for misjudgments.

Once I do this, I can move on, clearly seeing what I have to offer myself and others. With my blinders removed, I see my strengths as well as my weaknesses. I can also see how I am a part of the world around me, and, as part of the human race, I will see my responsibility to live with respect for all life.

Belief in Myself

You cannot now subdue me—
I am becoming stronger,
I am stronger, stronger, stronger.
        —*Iroquois poem,* "Magic Formula"

Part of my recovery is to claim pride in my culture. There may be challenges in the ways I am different and similar to others, but I will make every effort to live to my fullest by developing abilities to look at life's bigger picture.

In the face of adversity and injustice, I can still choose to believe in life and its fullest possibilities. In recovery, I have discovered my gratitude for choosing to believe in myself and for reaching out to others. I will use new tools to move ahead.

Earth

Part of It All

...where we had thought to travel outward, we shall come to the center of our own existence; where we had thought to be alone, we shall be with all the world.

—*Joseph Campbell,* Hero with a Thousand Faces

As I grow in love and acceptance for myself, I gain an increasingly deeper understanding of who I am. I have learned how worthy I am, how special I am. At the same time, the more I acknowledge my own uniqueness, the more I understand how much I am like others.

The wonder and gratitude I feel for my recovery reflect my appreciation of the lives around me. The strength I gain from feeling whole reflects the strength I draw from my connection with all living things. Knowing I am part of the whole helps me heal. My healing, in turn, allows me to help those around me heal.

Fear

Sometimes I sits and thinks, and sometimes I just sits.
—anonymous

On my path of recovery, I learn to listen to my heart. When I sense fear, one reaction I may have is the urge to run in the opposite direction. By facing my fears, I am entering the unknown.

If I stop and look rather than run away, and use and trust all my senses to review where I am, my fear and the situation will both seem more manageable. By facing my fears, I can learn to separate which ones are based on past experience and which fears are of new experiences.

Earth

Connection to the Sacred

Prayer from the heart can achieve what nothing else can in the world.
—Mohandas Gandhi

When I need a heart to heart connection with the Author of Peace, I pray. For me, this is returning to the source. Shutting out the distractions of the world and turning off all of my inner voices help me to focus on my connection to the sacred.

I have clarity of vision when I am heart to heart with the sacred. Ambiguities drop away and I experience wholeness. Prayer reaffirms my faith that I am making choices which are fitting for me.

Reassurance from Within

There are no guarantees.
From the viewpoint of fear
none are strong enough.
From the viewpoint of love
none are necessary.
   —Emmanuel's Book II, *compiled by Pat*
Rodegast and Judith Stanton

  When I am anxious and afraid, I naturally want reassurance. Reassurance comes from inside. I can draw courage from belief in myself and in my ideals, and from my faith in our Creator.

  In the face of fear, I can call on God to help guide me in my decisions. I can remind myself to trust myself, and to let go of what I cannot control. Returning to my center of love and faith, I am safe.

Earth

Being Alone

on a cold night
i forget the story of my birth
i forget the long fingers of sleep
the magic of names
to go alone
i begin by asking the winds
forgiveness.
        —*Lance Henson,* "Solitary"

Being alone differs from isolation. When I am alone I will remember my total being, that I am a part of a rich culture and heritage, a part of nature, one with the earth.

Sometimes in my alone times, I will identify, accept and work on my shortcomings. I can examine myself, and admit when I make a mistake as I settle my past to meet the present. In my self-searching, I can turn to myself, to others, or to the elements of the universe for grace and forgiveness.

Self-Definition

Self-pity in its early stages is as snug as a feather mattress. Only when it hardens does it become uncomfortable.
—Maya Angelou

Every day I make choices to define my place in the world. When I choose to eat healthful foods, I am defining myself as a person who loves and respects my physical being. When I choose to learn the history of my family, my culture, or of the country of my family origin, I am defining myself as someone who is proud of my ancestry.

My daily choices also define who I am spiritually and emotionally. I can choose to let go of resentment over past injustices and further my recovery by living in love and forgiveness. The choices I make today will reflect my self-definition as a person who stands for justice, love and forgiveness.

Feeling Fully

...for neither
happiness nor hurt
define life.
They merely
are two
of its diverse
elements
I merely live
　　—*Ricardo Sanchez,* Brown Bear Honey
Madness: Alaskan Cruising Poems

　　Serenity is created while having a full range of feelings within me. They reflect my vulnerability and my vitality as a human being. When I am angry or hurt by injustices, I can remain aware that I am capable of many other feelings as well.

　　The wounds of injustice do not deny my identity. I can use adverse experiences to renew my self-confidence and inner strengths. Part of spiritual growth comes from recognizing gratitude and serenity as a foundation of recovery.

51

Letting Go

All my ways of being are musical and mysterious.
Yet I embrace you openly.
Ripe with expectancy.
        —*Maya Angelou,* Now Sheba Sings the
Song

I believe in the process of my life as it unfolds. Just as the fallen leaf is still a part of the tree, I can trust and let go as I grow. If letting go feels uncertain, I will have faith in myself and others whom I trust.

Letting go—making a decision to live spiritually and turn my will and my life over to the care of God—results in personal breakthroughs and discovery. The self-knowledge and discoveries I find in recovery are strengthened as I blend my personal beliefs with the traditions and beliefs of my culture.

Always Listening

Dear Mr. God,
I think about you sometimes even when I'm not
praying.
        —Children's Letters to God, *compiled*
by Stuart Hample and Eric Marshall

Prayer is personal. As I heal, I have learned how to expand my definition of prayer. I can respect the way others express their devotion to their god or guiding spirit without making judgments or comparing it to how I pray.

I know that prayer can be in the form of dreams, drawings, song, writing and expressions of love. I will remember that direct communication between me and my Creator is possible at any time because we are always in contact. I know the Creator is always listening.

Act

Do it now, if you see what needs doing, do it.
　　—*Dhyani Ywahoo,* Voices of Our Ancestors

The further along in my recovery I am, the greater is my desire to continue growing. In the past, my fears caused me to hesitate, doubt my abilities and desires, and deny responsibilities. Now I meet these fears with action.

I know I have the power to control my actions and reactions. I know I can choose to act even if I am afraid. Accepting responsibility even as I dream my dreams can lead me to opportunities I otherwise would not see. Today I will take the action necessary to continue my recovery.

Living in the Present

The great artist is the simplifier.
  —*Henri Amiel*

Today is a new day for standing in the present, just where I am. Although I may see the paths in front of me, I will walk those when tomorrow comes. For now, the future is yet to be created, and the past has happened and cannot be changed.

An important lesson of my recovery is to heal from the events of past, to no longer dwell on conditions which may have been unsafe or unfair. I choose which path to walk as each day arrives. Of the many paths unfolding before me, I make sure I am on the road of peace.

Blending

It just seems clear to me that as long as we are all here, it's pretty clear that the struggle is to share the planet, rather than divide it.
—*Alice Walker*

Hundreds of years ago, the people who lived on this earth had plenty of room to roam. Differences in customs evolved from the lifestyles necessary to survive in a particular part of the world. We live much closer to each other today. As a result, we are offered the opportunity to learn about other ways of living and find out the value of diversity.

We are given the opportunity to create a lifestyle that honors our mix of traditions without diluting them. Today I honor my culture's traditions as well as those of others. I look for opportunities to use them for the greatest good.

Earth

Reading the Signals

We cannot put off living until we are ready.
The most salient characteristic of life is its
coerciveness: it is always urgent, "here and
now" without any possible postponement. Life
is fired at us point blank.
    —*José Ortega y Gasset*

In my recovery, I will listen to my body and
my spirit. My body and my spirit give me signals
when I am beginning to slide off track.

On another scale, nature also gives us signals
that our actions are risky. The hole in the ozone
and the decimation of certain wildlife species are
strong signals that we need to pay more attention
to the world around us. I will acknowledge my
connection to all of life by respecting and paying
heed to my inner signals and to nature's warning
signs.

Getting in Touch with Common Sense

An unusual amount of common sense is sometimes called wisdom.
—anonymous

My behavior is directly related to the way I think. In our beginnings, we all have a natural self-esteem, a natural joy and serenity. As we age, thought becomes more a part of us, and society and family influences become louder.

As a result, common sense and serenity may be smothered and harder to hear. Today I remember that in my recovery, my common sense is yet another way the Eternal Presence speaks to me. The thoughts, ideas, and beliefs I develop in recovery express themselves in my outer reality.

Earth

Kindness

Straight is my path.
Straight is my mind.
Straight is my heart.
Kind I will be to my brothers and sisters.
Kind I will be to beast and bird.
    —*Ojibway Song, translated by Basil*
Johnston, Ojibway Ceremonies

Selective kindness is like a tire with a slow leak. Perhaps it is not too noticeable at first, but it becomes a chronic problem until the leak is repaired. If I try to be kind to only some people some of the time, I will get back as little as I have given.

Partial kindness is an energy drain because it imposes limitations. When I am centered in love, kindness is a natural byproduct. I give it freely to all living things, including the earth itself.

The Spring Garden

You have forgiven the world today. You can look upon it now as if you never saw it before.
—Foundation for Inner Peace, A Course in Miracles

In the Spring, lilac buds unfurl as last year's plants work their way up through rotting leaves and branches. There is no greater encouragement for hope and renewal than Spring. I also have my own regeneration cycle. To make sure I thrive, I will keep my inner environment clean of weeds and poisons.

My seasons may not be as orderly as Mother Nature's, but I have the good fortune of being able to schedule Spring whenever I need it. I can choose to put my past hurts and resentments behind me and send up new shoots of growth. My friends and family, my culture, my values and beliefs are my root system, providing nourishment and security. With loving care, my garden

Sun

vitality

Sun

Strength

The ultimate aim of the human mind, in all its efforts, is to become acquainted with Truth.
—*Eliza Farnham,* Woman and Her Era

To begin my recovery, I faced the shadow side of my psyche. I had to acknowledge parts of me which may have led to poor judgment or unhealthy choices. However, acceptance of my shadow self does not cause that part of me to up and disappear. By accepting it, though, I am stronger.

I can now trust myself completely, and not try to hide anything anymore. Also, acknowledging my own failings helps me understand and tolerate those of others. Accepting all parts of myself helps me be forgiving of myself and of others.

Balance

The art of progress is to preserve order amid change and to preserve change amid order.
—*Alfred North Whitehead*

My healing is a balancing act. While working to change harmful habits, I am continually pushing forward toward my dreams. I am also taking care of myself by making sure I get enough rest, eat good food and leave myself time to play. To stay balanced I need to listen to my body.

Taking time to reflect on and acknowledge my changes can also help me stay balanced. My recovery is a lifelong journey which can only be made day by day. Today I will take the time to acknowledge my accomplishments. Knowing that maintaining balance will keep me in shape for my journey, I will nourish any neglected parts of my life.

Sun

A Sacred Act

Every person is a human being. Every human personality is sacred, potentially divine. Nobody is any more than that and nobody can be less.
—*Margaret Walker Alexander*

Recovery leads me to appreciation of the sacredness of life. Thinking about the sacred does not mean I must just stop and reflect for long periods of time on icons or symbols which have been deemed sacred. And it means more than going to a place of worship or reading books of inspiration.

I can feel the sacredness of life in any activity when I am fully present in the moment. At times, silent meditation, books of inspiration, or group rituals are how I acknowledge the sacred. Other times, my most ordinary tasks are most sacred.

Purposeful Actions

*Life is to be lived, not controlled, and humanity
is won by continuing to play in face of certain
defeat.*
  —*Ralph Ellison,* The Invisible Man

  In my recovery, I turn my life over to my God.
I do this willingly, and with thanks. Trusting my
Creator to guide my life does not, however, mean
I live without a sense of purpose.

  My healing and joy come from living a
meaningful life, a life which reflects who I am, my
values, my ideals. As I take time each day to listen
to my heart, my purpose becomes clearer and my
sense of place in the world stronger.

Sun

Staying Connected

Alone, all alone
Nobody, but nobody
Can make it out here alone.
        —*Maya Angelou,* Oh Pray My Wings
Are Gonna Fit Me Well

In my recovery I recognize and value the importance of staying connected to myself, to others, and to my spirituality. When I draw on my courage to trust myself and others, I nourish feelings of harmony and sharing. I will keep an open mind as I turn to myself and to others for support.

The reflections and suggestions of my program of recovery can give me courage to seek and stay connected to what I believe. Listening and giving and receiving are the threads of staying connected.

Asking

Wise friends are the best book of life, because they teach with voice and looks.
    —*Calderón de la Barca,* "The Secret in Words"

I am not alone. There are others who share my values and my ideals. Together we can support each other in our healing and in living our ideals. I know I am loved and honored, and others will be there for me when I need to lean on them.

At the same time, I recognize I am strong and have much to give others when they are in distress. I know asking for help takes strength. Today I will ask for help if I need to. I will also let others know that I can offer them the support and help they may need, and do it lovingly and gratefully.

Sun

My Own Answers

First learn to love yourself, then you can love me.
—*St. Bernard of Clairvaux,* Letters

Sometimes I may find myself in a pattern of trying too hard. I might look in vain for symbolic or grand events to guide my decisions. Or I might get ahead of myself and try to find an answer before I have fully identified the problem.

When I am confused, I can ask myself if I am making the situation more complicated than it needs to be. Am I missing the obvious? In the most basic sense, what is my immediate need? I can use the tools of my program of recovery to find clarity.

Love Yourself

i found god in myself
& i loved her/i loved her fiercely.
> —*Ntozake Shange,* "for colored girls
> who have considered suicide/when the rainbow
> is enuf"

I am as I need to be. In the past, my behavior
may have been destructive. In the future, I may
make a mistake. But I am as I need to be. In my
dealings with others and in thinking about myself, I know the importance of separating the
action from the person.

The hurting child may be present in me
today. When I feel vulnerable or ashamed, I can
try to find the source. If it is old messages, I can
take time to comfort myself, to reassure myself.
I can hold myself and others accountable for
actions without making judgments of essential
goodness or unworthiness.

Sun

Just Being

Lift up yourselves...take yourselves out of the mire and hitch your hopes to the stars.
   —*Marcus Garvey,* Philosophy and Opinions

When a newborn baby yawns, it is a full body event. From fingertip to toe, eyebrows to heel, she holds back not at all. But for me, yawning is something I usually do while thinking about something else. With each passing year, there are more day to day tasks that I do by habit, without focusing my attention on them.

On occasion, though, I am reminded of the luxury of just being. Of not planning for tomorrow's meeting, not striving to finish one task as quickly as possible to move on to the next. Today I will live in the luxury of the moment.

vitality

Speak Out

Most of us are proud of our freedom to say what we please. What we wish we had is the courage to say it.

> *—from the magazine* Bits and Pieces, *Feb. 6, 1992*

Sometimes a new way of thinking or being seems fragile, easily blown away in the face of a hurtful remark. When I am hesitant about whether to speak out, I can ask myself if this feeling comes from my own questions about my position, or from fear of the opinions of others.

If I talk the talk but do not walk the walk, I risk undermining my trust in myself and diminishing self-confidence. Action based in belief in myself and my values is empowering. Today I will provide a safe and nurturing environment for my efforts to change by speaking out.

Mind

I don't let my mouth say nothin' my head can't stand.
—*Louis Armstrong*

When my mind is free of theories and false concepts, all forms of beauty and abundance present themselves to me. I recognize that I have a voice in what happens to me. The tools of recovery teach me to know my feelings and thoughts, and to speak from my heart. The more open I am to this understanding, the more I witness recovery and life's flow.

vitality

Good At Heart

I still believe that people are really good at heart. I simply can't build up my hopes on a foundation consisting of confusion, misery and death.

—Anne Frank, The Diary of Anne Frank

Despite the atrocities some individuals commit against others, my healing grows from a belief in the basic goodness of life. I can reinforce that belief by truly seeing the daily miracles around me—the beauty of nature, the compassion and joy of my friends, the power of my own ability to change.

Elements of life such as these are not to be taken for granted. By knowing joy in the daily workings of life, I can find strength to face the threatening sides of humanity. And, as I have learned in facing my own shadows, the very act of naming the elements that threaten weakens them.

Sun

True Words

To pray
is to know how to stand still
and to dwell upon a word.
  -*Abraham Heschel,* I Asked for Wonder

Knowing how powerful words are, I try not to let them fall out of my mouth without thought. Today I will make an extra effort to think about and listen to what I am saying. I will pay close attention, and revise the harmful messages that I give myself and others.

These messages may be in the form of cynical humor or self-pressure, such as thoughts phrased as 'shoulds,' 'have tos,' and 'not enoughs.' Today I will speak and think positively. I will reinforce my recovery by turning off the dribbling faucet— words with little thought behind them.

vitality

Speak the Truth

May your sight be as straight as an arrow, and may all your arrows aim at Truth.
    —*Mary Summer Rain,* Spirit Song

To speak the truth, I must first see truth. Working through denial so that I can recognize what is true is an important part of my growth. At times this has been challenging.

I can remind myself of the truth of my recovery. Affirmations, lists of successes, support meetings and writing are all ways I can keep truth in front of me. Every act of truthfulness reinforces my recovery.

Sun

Asking for Help

To know the road ahead, ask those coming back.
—Chinese proverb

There are many people who have much to teach me and who are more than willing to assist me on my journey. Often their desire to help comes from the help they received themselves. Accepting responsibility for my own actions includes being able to ask for help.

I know it is a sign of strength to seek assistance or guidance when I am feeling uncertain or isolated. As we all learn to give and accept help from others, we build an empowered community. Today I can ask for, and gratefully accept, help from others.

Inner Self

...give me beauty in the inward soul; and may the outward and inward person be at one.
—*Plato*

The meshing of my inner and outer self is at the core of my healing. My inner, private self keeps me going. It guides my decisions and nourishes my spirit. My outer, public self acts on my decisions and choices, and determines how I am seen in the world. With these two together, I am whole.

As I take steps to realize my dreams, I need all parts of myself to work towards my greatest good. Through self-maintenance, I will keep all parts up and running, providing myself with good food, exercise, and rest. I accept myself as whole, and I respect myself.

The Person Behind the Mask

There's a period of life when we swallow a knowledge of ourselves and it becomes either good or sour inside.
—Pearl Bailey

When I remove my masks, I am faced with all my weaknesses and character flaws. As I heal, however, I learn what I once judged as a weakness or a character flaw is often a reaction born of hurt or shame. When those feelings are turned inward, my very existence is threatened.

My path in recovery is to integrate all parts of me, to cherish myself and become whole. In the face of adversities, I can choose to believe in myself. I can choose self-love and acceptance.

vitality

Ways of Seeing

Only as you know yourself can your brain serve you as a sharp and efficient tool. Know your own failings, passions, and prejudices so you can separate them from what you see.
—*Bernard M. Baruch*

My perceptions filter through my experiences, my cultural traditions, and my value system. I can make sure my perceptions of others are fair by being honest about my prejudices, by learning more about other cultural traditions, and by basing my decisions in love.

If I am mindful of the influences on my way of seeing, I will treat others fairly. Although I cannot change how others think or feel, I can be open and willing to show by example how to respect and honor differences.

Sun

Giving

You must learn to say no when something is not right for you.
    —*Leontyne Price*

There will be times when I have more to give to others, and times when I have to pull back to take care of myself. Self-care is not an act of selfishness. It is a necessity for ensuring that what I have to give will grow stronger and deeper.

Learning more about my personal boundaries, I will define what I need to keep myself centered. And I know that those parameters will change. Knowing my personal limits and giving of my time and self to others are important parts of recovery.

Love Free and Clear

*Love does not consist in gazing at each other
(one perfect sunrise gazing at another!) but in
looking outward together in the same direction.*
—Antoine Saint-Exupéry

In the movies, love is often portrayed as a
magnet, an attraction between two people which
is so intense that nothing else matters. Magnets
have a tendency to attract many elements, however, and false expectations or intertwined resentments can come from this "magnetic" form of
love.

As I heal, I learn the importance of love given
free and clear. Love which is honored, rather
than judged, deepens even as it expands. Together, the giver and the receiver of free and clear
love become magnets for goodness. Today I will
give love unconditionally to myself and to others.

Sun

Plumes of Friendship

Like a quetzal plume, a fragrant flower,
friendship sparkles:
like heron plumes, it weaves itself into finery.
— "Friendship," *an Aztec poem*

Today I will celebrate friendship, waving it high like the finest of heron plumes. I am grateful for the loving support I receive and give to my friends and family. I delight in their humor, and give thanks for their compassion and ability to forgive.

I will value our differences and strive to understand our varying experiences. Together, my friends, my family and I move into the world, strong in our love, our integrity, and our commitment to one another.

Have a Dream

I have a dream that my four little children will one day live in a nation where they will not be judged by the color of their skin, but by the content of their character.
—*Martin Luther King, Jr.*

When I am feeling threatened and alone, I can look to the dreams and words of others to inspire me. I can follow their leadership in summoning courage and taking action, in creating possibilities for myself by living by my ideals. Thousands upon thousands of people keep Martin Luther King's dream alive by keeping it with them every day.

His cry for justice alone could not make people change their behavior, but the lives of those spent acting on their beliefs shows us how change can be brought about. In looking to the dreams and wisdom of others, I can enrich and realize my own dreams.

Sun

Rewards

You're not obligated to win. You're obligated to keep trying to keep doing the best you can every day.
—*Marian Wright Edelman*

Today there is a growing expectation that people will give more when getting something in return. Incentives are offered across the board, from calendars given away for joining organizations to prizes given by schools for attendance and scholarly achievement. We place emphasis on results, missing a basic appreciation for the value of the process.

When I try to do the best I can, no matter what my end goal is, I experience the sacredness of the moment. My complete participation gives me a sense of deep involvement and satisfaction which flows throughout the rest of my day, and perhaps even longer. Today I will do my best, and let that be its own reward.

vitality

Joyful Living

*I could feel creation, myself in place
for the first time.*
    —*Sharon Doubiago,* South America
Mi Hija

In my recovery I am striving to make every day meaningful. When I am on track and centered, everything runs smoothly. No matter what the weather, it is a perfect day. No matter how much money I have, it is the right amount.

Today I know that I am in the right place at the right time. I trust myself to make choices that reflect my ideals and nurture my spirit. I accept myself unconditionally and live my life with joy.

Sun

Love

It is sad not to be loved, but it is much sadder not to be able to love.
   —Miguel Unamuno

As I heal, I can let love into my life, and give and receive it freely. My love and full feeling for life are catalysts to celebrate and affirm my identity. Rather than fear the fullness of my feelings, I can embrace the freedom they give me.

In my love for life I can allow myself new discoveries and stay open to exploration, learning about myself and those whom I love. I can also open myself for others to know me. As I practice loving myself more, I am better able to love others and to receive the love given me.

Room to Give

I run to help you, are you okay?
One arm lifts yours and you say
you slipped.

　　　　—Nellie Wong, "For A Woman Who Has Fallen"

　　　Today I will open my heart to those in need, and open my hand to giving. No matter how full my life is, I will leave room to give aid to someone in need. Whatever color, creed or gender, all people are part of the human race.

　　　We all have hopes and dreams, pain and fear. We all need a helping hand at times. By giving, I can become more accepting of differing lifestyles, of different ways of being.

In the Right Place

Dear God,
It is great the way you always get the stars in the
right places.
> —Children's Letters to God, *compiled*
> *by Stuart Hample and Eric Marshall*

Today I will accept that I am in the right place. I know I have all I need for living my life fully and joyfully. My experiences are what I need, and so are the people around me.

I give thanks for the world around me, recognizing that the universe provides me with opportunities and nourishment to heal and thrive. I embrace my changes and growth with love and acceptance.

Goodwill

Flowers leave some of their fragrance in the hand that bestows them.
—Chinese proverb

As I learn to give of myself lovingly and without expectation, traces of my goodwill linger and enrich my being. From this foundation of goodness rise my sense of self and a sense of who I am in the world. I can affirm my willingness to grow in my recovery by valuing the differences of those around me and respecting the physical world in which we all live.

Moon
cycles

Moon

Ups and Downs

If one month is long, another month is short.
Comment: Life has its ups and downs.
  —Maxims and Proverbs of Old Korea,
translated by Tae Hung Ha

Life consists of cycles. I embrace the challenges of these cycles, just as I embrace the joys and happiness they bring. While looking at the cycles of living, whether individual or global, I will acknowledge I can use the ups and downs as part of my growth and recovery.

I can learn to recognize patterns, and use these as lessons. One thing which helps me through challenging times is remembering that the depth of pain can be paralleled by the height of joy.

Dawn

When you get into a tight place and everything goes against you till it seems you could not hold on a minute longer, never give up then for that is just the place and time that the tide will turn.
—*Harriet Beecher Stowe*

When facing hardships, I can reflect on the parts of my life that bring joy. I remember that self-acceptance and self-worth cannot be destroyed from without. I accept that I do not have control over all the circumstances sur-rounding me, but I can control my own actions and beliefs.

Today I choose to treat both myself and others with respect, and to act honestly and with integrity. My faith supports me, even in the most turbulent times, as I move toward the dawning of a better day.

Moon

New Beginnings

Human rebirth has no end.
—Pablo Neruda

Recovery means new beginnings, and part of the healing nature of beginnings means accepting the past. Today I will acknowledge and embrace my past and the history and traditions of my culture and of my ancestors. I can accept the challenge of integrating my past into my present as part of my new beginning.

As I heal and begin anew, I search for trusted ground. Rather than fear the changes of beginnings, I can welcome each moment as it comes. I honor and celebrate myself and my recovery. I will meet today's experiences with self-confidence and trust.

Putting the Past
in Perspective

*The moon and the year
travel and pass away;
also the day, also the wind.*
        —"The Moon And The Year," *a Mayan
poem*

As I move ahead to find new ways in recovery, I can accept my personal past as I work on understanding the historical past of my people. I will remember I cannot control the past, for it is gone.

I am only in charge of my present life, responsible for my actions, thoughts and feelings. Today I will embrace my survival from the parts of my past that were harmful. In my recovery I am committed to cherishing freedom from the past.

Moon

Forgiveness

The relinquishment of anger and attack and the practice of forgiveness are essential to the realization of peace both in the world and in ourselves.

— *Foundation for Inner Peace,* A Course in Miracles

My recovery requires that I acknowledge my feelings, and then find constructive ways to work for change. When angered by unjust treatment, I may feel the urge for vengeance. Anger may be a healthy reaction to a destructive situation, but it is not the best basis for action. Hatred begets hatred, and creates a field of emotional quicksand.

Despite my feelings of anger, I know there are other responses beyond lashing out. I can choose to forego retaliation and stay out of the quicksand. I can take strong action to promote justice when I am grounded in forgiveness and integrity.

cycles

Cast Off the Past

Know that you will only move forward by casting useless things aside. Drop your worn out attitudes of the past. For there can be no progress until you change. As your thoughts become new, so do your circumstances.
—*Kristin Zambucka,* Keeper of the Earth

When I start feeling that I cannot move forward no matter how hard I try, I can stop and ask myself if I am being held back by issues from the past. Experience shows me that every time I face old beliefs and behavior and then let go of them, I can move freely into new territory.

Sometimes these ties to the past are veiled and hard to see for what they are. Even though I have acknowledged and accepted that many things from my past have caused me problems, I am still surprised and frustrated when they reappear in different forms. It may take several efforts to cast off the past, but I know each effort strengthens my commitment to recovery.

Sacred Guidance

For what has been—thanks!
For what shall be—yes!
　　—Dag Hammarskjöld

As I renew my connection with the sacred, I am grateful for life. Every stage of life triggers new possibilities which will lead to even more possibilities. Understanding that life offers me what I am willing to take, I look forward to receiving its gifts every day.

Along the way, it can be difficult to accept the pain as well as the joy of honest self-evaluation and personal discovery. I can trust my instincts and joyfully carry a touch of sacredness throughout the day.

How Do We Treat One Another?

Man in the store ask me what I done in this life to get to be so old. I say, 'Treatin' people right, and having good thoughts of people, and trust in God.' If you do the right thing in this world and treat people right, right will follow you.
　　—Lula Bell Mack, from One Hundred Over 100, *compiled and edited by Jim Heynen*

Recovery teaches me to treat others in ways in which I like to be treated. When something went wrong, I used to look around for someone to blame. Troubles can be just troubles, instead of being someone's fault.

I can choose to separate the action from the person, and show compassion while still holding someone accountable for their actions. As I make room for the Eternal Presence in my life, I make room for my own mistakes and those of others.

Moon

Challenges Bring Gifts

*Moons wane when their brightest rays fade.
Comment: In nature and human events there
are ups and downs in life like the phases of the
moon: after joy comes grief and bitter goes
before sweet.*
> —Maxims and Proverbs of Old Korea,
> *translated by Tae Hung Ha*

The illumination which comes in my recovery dissolves the mist that can hinder my view of the horizon. Some of this haze comes from my frustration about lack of equality as I perceive it, from injustices involving myself or others.

In some way, however, challenge is also a gift. I can ask myself, "What am I afraid of? What is the worst thing that could possibly happen?" If I choose to be afraid for a moment, fine. I can experience a full range of feelings in recovery. I am deserving of the best of all things possible.

Embrace This Day

Life is what we make it, always has been, always will be.
—*Grandma Moses*

Yesterdays may have been bound in fear and hurt, but tomorrows are hopes not yet arrived. I will embrace this day as all I have. Living in the present releases me to hope for change and growth. As I change in my recovery, my relationship with my culture and its traditions may change.

Rather than fearing those changes, I will welcome each moment as it comes. I honor my own growth and diversity. I honor the diversity of other people and their opinions and attitudes. I will meet today's experiences with self-confidence and trust. I celebrate my transformations.

Moon

Respect

Honor the light in all. Compare nothing; see all for its suchness. Respect all life; cut away ignorance from one's own heart...
     —*Dhyani Ywahoo,* Voices of Our Ancestors

If I look at situations as win or lose, I lose no matter what. By accepting the concept of a "loser," I buy into a misleading image that exists in our society. I can choose not to look at someone as less than someone else. I can choose to honor and respect all life.

Soaring

*As long as you keep a person down, some part
of you has to be down there to hold the person
down, so it means you cannot soar as you
otherwise might.*
　—*Marian Anderson*

It takes energy to expect the worst. I try not
to limit my imagination, to shut off untold possibilities. When my expectations are open to all
possibilities, they generate an energy of their
own.

The same is true of how I treat others. If I
expect someone to disappoint me, then I have
to be on the lookout for proof that I was right.
Today I will choose to expect the best and open
myself up to the possibilities.

Moon

Precious Life

The opportunity of life is very precious, and it moves very quickly.
—Dhyani Ywahoo, Voices of Our Ancestors

It is possible to miss opportunities for enjoyment and enrichment if we are too concerned with the passing of time. Computers that were science fiction thirty years ago are now used by pre-schoolers; global communication systems beam information around the world in minutes. These advancements can be used to free up time for us, but some people use them to schedule their lives for weeks and weeks ahead. Today I will focus on whatever I am doing at the moment. I will grasp what life offers me by giving every present moment my full attention.

Shine

The capacity for grief is as much from God as the capacity for love—and we have not really lived until we have sounded them both.
—anonymous

I can choose joy. I may have faced many hardships, and I know I have not seen the last of them in my life. But I can choose to reinforce the joy in my life by treating myself with love and respect.

In the daily miracles which are all around me, I can choose to find contentment and inspiration. Life is not without pain, but how pain and hardship affect my life is up to me.

Endings

Are we to look at cherry blossoms only in full bloom, the moon only when it is cloudless? To long for the moon while looking on the rain...[this is] even more deeply moving.
—*Yoshida Kenko,* Essays in Idleness

An ending is always the start of a new beginning, just as the end of the season can be cause for welcoming the new season. Endings mean loss only if I decide they do.

An ending provides memories to cherish, stories to be passed along to others, moments to be replayed and savored. The past becomes a part of me that I can call on whenever I choose.

Openness

Invest in the human soul. Who knows, it might be a diamond in the rough.
—Mary McLeod Bethune, from an address delivered September 21, 1926

Although my past may be marked by pain, pride, joy or sorrow, today I will be open to loving others and allowing myself to be loved. I can honor my experiences, my history, and the traditions of my culture by welcoming growth and change into my life.

My openness is a way of loving myself, allowing me to maintain and cherish my distinct identity. Recovery promotes and inspires change within me, and transition is preceded by taking risks and being open. Today I am open to letting someone know me.

Moon

Questions

*The journey of a thousand miles must begin
with a single step.*
—*Lao-Tze,* The Way of Lao-Tze

Even though I sometimes take a stray turn, I
know my journey of recovery is basically on
track. It is guided by faith in my Source of Peace,
and in trust I feel in myself.

I can restrain myself from second-guessing
my decisions or questioning my choices. I can
review my choices in recovery and recall that
the outcome is worth striving for.

Sharing Experiences

Cuando sientes que tu hermana no necessita de tu amor. No le cierres tus entranas ni el calor del corazón. (When you feel that your brothers and sisters need a start, don't contain all your affections, nor the warmth that's in your heart.)
—from the spiritual "Gloria, Gloria, Aleluya!"

By sharing my experiences in recovery, I am less likely to feel isolated, different or alienated. It is healthy to acknowledge differences while also exploring similarities, and to remember my hopes, strengths and ideas are worthwhile.

By sharing my experiences, I can realize their full meaning and learn from what I have in common with others. Change is preceded by taking risks. Today I am open to letting someone know me.

Common Ground

...the intimate face of the universal struggle.
You begin with your family and the kids on the
block, and next you open your eyes to what you
call your people...
    —*June Jordan,* Civil Wars

Social change begins with individual change. To help create a world in which freedom for all is the reality, I have no choice but to start with me, with what I can control. Treating myself with dignity and respect acknowledges the value of who I am as a person.

Accepting my weaknesses helps me to keep from expecting others to be perfect. Learning about my cultural traditions gives me perspective and a more complete sense of my identity. When I do these things, being true to myself becomes the only possible course.

cycles

Stay With It

Revolution begins with the self, in the self.
        —Toni Cade Bambara, from a lecture given in December 1965

When the sheer enormity of the injustices in the world hit me in the face, I may think, "Why bother to keep trying?" This is a signal for me to stop and take stock of how far I have come on my personal journey. I can also draw strength from my pride in those who have struggled before me.

History shows me again and again how courageous people have taken great risks and succeeded against seemingly impossible odds. As I visualize the women and men, young and old, who would not give up on making the world better for all of us, their vitality lifts my spirit and their voices urge me to take heart and try again.

The Circle of Being

The way to do is to be.
  —Lao-Tze

There are too many interesting things to do in my life. My "to do" list will never be finished. And the more I learn, the more things I find I want to pursue. But a list of desires does not bring me spiritual or emotional fulfillment. My emotional strength and spiritual grounding come from acceptance of myself, and from my connection to the world.

When I accept and love myself, I can trust my very being. This trust and self-love leads me, in turn, to venture out and live in joy. I am open to those around me. And the more I love and learn, the more I am centered in my spirit.

Opportunity from Cultural Influences

Challenges make you discover things about yourself that you never really knew. They're what make the instrument stretch—what make you go beyond the norm.
—Cicely Tyson

My inner and outer identities are harmonized by my search for growth. Just as I can examine the relationships in my family without judgment, so I am free to explore how cultural influences have affected my behavior.

All of the cultural influences in my life have a bearing on each moment of my recovery, on each moment I live. My recovery means appreciating my identity. I now acknowledge past wounds, and I accept this challenge and the courage it demands as part of my recovery.

Potential

As soon as I hear a name, I feel convinced I can guess what the owner looks like, but it never happens when I actually meet the person that their face is as I had supposed.
— *Yoshida Kenko,* Essays in Idleness

I prefer people to respond to who I am, rather than to who they think I am. One way I can encourage people to do this is by returning the act in kind. I will be true to myself and my recovery by refraining from snap judgments about people based on what I hear about them, or on their name, race, weight, height, style of dress, or any other outward display.

cycles

Lead the Way

Our deeds determine us as much as we determine our deeds.
—*George Elliot*, Adam Bede

I can be a leader by living a lifestyle which is as true to my ideals as possible. I can show others that differences in skin color, economic class, religion or sexual preference need not be barriers.

I can show others the value of cultural diversity by honoring it myself. When my actions are based in love, I become one of many who can lead the way to a better world.

Connected

Enjoy whatever you see of nature that we didn't create. Look at the sky! Look at the clouds! Look at the water! Look at the trees! I say, 'Be grateful.'

—David Kane, from One Hundred Over 100, *compiled and edited by Jim Heynen*

Staying connected to the earth and to nature helps keep me connected to my Creator. All of nature speaks to us. The more I am open to the messages of the universe, the more I hear the trees, the wind, the rain.

Life is similar to the cycle of the full moon. Just as I am aware of the whole cycle of the moon's waxing and waning, I recognize my own transitions and evolution.

Goodbyes

When one door of happiness closes another opens; but often we look so long at the closed door that we do not see the one which has been opened for us.
—*Helen Keller*

In our growth, we touch and realize spirituality within each of us. Sometimes goodbyes enhance our spiritual flowering. In saying goodbye to habits of the old me, I can allow space for a wiser me to freely express itself. And in gaining this fresh expression, I can allow others to travel their own roads.

Passages

Every exit is an entry somewhere else.
        —Tom Stoppard

Some of us thought that when we grew up we would understand the purpose of life, what the point of it all is. Even as an adult, I may have hoped for "the ultimate moment"—the one event or feeling or observation which would be the pinnacle, the point at which I could finally say, "Oh! I get it!"

As I move from one stage of my life into the next, I accept that all stages are of value. Each stage of my life offers me opportunities for loving, learning and laughing.

cycles

Today

Beyond the mountains there are more mountains again.
—*Haitian proverb*

Time is like the slippery slope of a high mountain. The past may seem like a long slide, beyond the broken branches and crumbled ledges of my "if onlys" and "should haves," down to the rocks of despair below. And the future may appear to be a sheer, glass-smooth wall, rising an unknown distance into swirling mist.

None of that treacherous expanse is any good for climbing. There is a solid ledge, though, which is called "today." Wounds, scars, or resentments from yesterday can burden the present, where I am trying to live with forgiveness, wisdom and well-being. So long as I keep my footing in today, I am perfectly safe.

Animals
wisdom

Inner Wisdom

I am my life. And only mine. And so I shall appreciate my person. And so I shall make proper use of my self.
—*Ruth Beebe Hill,* Hanto Yo

My search for happiness, love, and peace of mind may have caused me to look outside myself at times. When I practice stilling my mind, I can open myself to hear the inner wisdom that is with me always.

Serenity allows me to access my wisdom. When my mind is quiet I begin to see life more objectively. By being honest with myself, respect and love for myself and others grows. I can release my true essence.

Authenticity

Peace of mind is clearly an internal matter. It must begin with your own thoughts, and then extend outward. It is from your peace of mind that a peaceful perception of the world arises.
—*Foundation for Inner Peace,* A Course in Miracles

It is easy to come up with a list of things I "should" do. Experience has shown me, though, that when I start thinking in terms of "shoulds," my motivation strays from my authentic self.

When my inner "should" voice starts up, I can stop it by centering myself and examining old messages. It may be that I decide to take action, but the action will be based on my true values.

Hold Your Center

I had crossed the line. I was free; but there was no one to welcome me to the land of freedom. I was a stranger on a strange land.
—Harriet Tubman

Trust is vital in my recovery. When I am feeling overwhelmed, I will trust myself that I am on the best path. When I am feeling shaky and vulnerable, I might want things to be clear cut, without uncertainties.

I can remember that faith is important as I try turning over my uncertainties to the Source of my being and hope. I trust that my center will hold, just as I hold my faith in the Source of Peace.

Trusting My Inner Self

....now I can serenely walk,
seek meaning
(whatever that means)
and caress the breezes...
    —*Ricardo Sanchez,* Brown Bear Honey
Madness: Alaskan Cruising Poems

I can seek my own meaning and sense of purpose in life by drawing on my inner self. As it guides me, I will discover my courage and ability to trust myself and others. If I stand in the midst of injustice or inequities, I can choose to reflect on and remember a larger picture of life.

Trusting my serenity and courage will carry me through difficult experiences, and will highlight the joyous times of life as well. Today I will take at least one moment for reflection, to quiet my mind and body, my thoughts and actions, and to seek serenity by experiencing my inner self.

Courage

Courage is not freedom from fear; it is being afraid and going on.
        —anonymous

Experience has shown me that fear of the unknown diminishes when I trust myself and my convictions. Even though fear may tell me to turn and run, today I can resolve to move ahead. I can face fears and go forward, for each time I face my fears, I strengthen my ability to live in joy.

Fear of known adversaries is also weakened when I stand firm in my belief of my value as a person. I will use the strength of my convictions to give me true courage.

Becoming Human

Becoming human means discovering our fullness and learning to live from it. This involves bringing forth more of who we really are and becoming more available to whatever life presents.
—*John Welwood,* Journey of the Heart

I delight in learning more about who I am. As I explore layer after layer, I learn not only about myself, but also about the joy of being human. As I glimpse the complexities of life, I realize it is not enough for me to just survive. I want to live fully and experience all life has to offer.

My belief in the sacredness of life gives my explorations meaning. I submerge myself in the possibilities of life, letting them color my dreams. The more I learn, the more I want to know. Today I honor the fullness of life and embrace the immensity of what the world can teach.

Possibilities

Sometimes it's worse to win a fight than to lose.
—Billie Holiday

When I recognize I have options and possibilities to choose from in life, I become freer. I can face each day with a choice and decision to do the best I can. Rather than judge myself with winning or losing, success or failure, prosperity or poverty, I will create my own definitions of success and winning. My commitment to honor my identity, my culture, and its traditions is a symbol of my success.

Goals

My only gift
is but an infinity
of human possibilities
limited only
by scant time
and enclosing spaces.
        —*Ricardo Sanchez,* Brown Bear Honey
Madness: Alaskan Cruising Poems

My recovery enriches my ability to strive for realistic goals. Knowing my limits frees me to expand and explore. Differences in skin color, culture, language, and ancestry combine into the richness of the human race, and accepting others does not deny my identity or diminish my goals. I can respect differences and embrace the diversity of others. Differences are treasures—to learn about, explore and accept.

Stories to Live By

The universe is made of stories, not of atoms.
—Muriel Rukeyser

People of all ages and cultures have valuable lessons to teach. The stories I learned as a child entertained me, but they also taught me how the world worked. I can continue to learn about the world by listening to and observing the stories around me.

Listening to others with an open mind and open heart can give me insight into the differences among us. Observing them live their stories can teach me about love and acceptance. Learning the traditions of my culture and those of others shows me our commonness even as we are distinct.

wisdom

A Laughing Matter

I know why the caged bird sings!
—*Paul Laurence Dunbar,* "Sympathy"

The more I am able to keep my sense of humor, the more I am able to keep centered on my healing. When things seem so difficult and I don't know whether to laugh or cry, I can choose either, for both are a relief. Laughing lightens my load and puts my problems into perspective. Humor shared with another helps break down misunderstandings and intolerance and helps build commonalities. Today laughter will come easily and often for me.

Discovery

In the sphere of all that we see, touch, hear, smell, taste, imagine and believe / there is a Sacred Space. And in that Sacred Space / there is a Temple of Reflection, a Temple of the Moon. And in the Temple of the Moon / there is a Shrine of Revelation / a Shrine of Understanding / a Shrine for the Flowering of the Heart.
—"Temple of the Moon," *author unknown*

Exploration, growth and acceptance are important elements of my recovery. I find there are infinite possibilities to choose from as I seek and set goals which are in harmony with my beliefs and integrity. I can achieve what I strive for. This discovery is a gift of my work in recovery.

Sharing

Isolation is the worst possible counselor.
  —*Miguel Unamuno*

Trust and knowledge are vital to my recovery, and as I learn to know and trust myself and others, I can share my thoughts, feelings and ideas. I am committed to letting others know my joys and sorrows, my anger, my love, my wants and needs.

By sharing dreams, hopes and aspirations with others, I acknowledge my desire to let people in. I am important to those who like and love me, and the people I love and like are meaningful to me. Today I am inspired to share.

Honoring Friends

Go often to the house of your friend; for weeds soon choke up the unused path.
—Scandinavian proverb

Friendships depend on give and take. Today I honor my friends, valuing them as individuals without taking them for granted. If I were to seek out my friends only when I needed their support or attention, I would be doing them and myself a disservice. I accept my friends for who they are, acknowledging our differences.

In turn, I offer my friends the opportunity to accept and appreciate who I am as an individual, and to witness the miracle of my recovery. Knowing good fellowship requires attention and nurturing. Today I will honor a friend by renewing our connection.

wisdom

Of Real Advantage

*Never esteem anything as of advantage to you
that will make you break your word or lose your
self-respect.*
   —*Marcus Aurelius Antoninus*

It would be nice to think that having started
my recovery, I will never waiver. But I know that
as I look at myself honestly, I will continue to find
behaviors and beliefs that will be difficult to let
go. However, I can go deeper and ask myself
what I can do to help me move ahead.

When I face such a challenge, I can ask
myself about the real value of what I am holding
onto. Whatever I find, I will make sure that I
nurture only what is of real advantage to me.

Wisdom Within

*Don't be satisfied with stories, how things have
gone with others. Unfold your own myth.*
—*Rumi,* Your Mythic Journey

When I remember the wondrous wisdom
within me, I feel a natural peace that accompanies it. If I have a day where my mood is low, I
need only to remember my natural wisdom. As
I understand myself more, I can see my own
innocence.

When I release self-judgment and condemnation, I also will try not to mistake internalized
myth for reality. Embracing all of myself, I gain
self-confidence, accepting myself just as I am.

Truth

...the truth has a strange way of following you, of coming up to you and making you listen to what it has to say.
—Sandra Cisneros, from the story "One Holy Night"

A truth is like a seed buried deep within the earth. With the right care, the seed anchors itself in Mother Earth and sends strong green shoots to the surface to thrive under the sun.

I can protect my own tender growth by trusting my inner wisdom and nurturing myself. I know the more I face the truth about myself and my fears, the easier it becomes to see and hear those truths. I anchor my truths in the rich foundation of self-esteem.

Tools of Recovery

"Don't worry about how it happens," he said. "There are many things you will never understand, but they happen anyway."
—*Tony Shearer,* The Praying Flute

Trust and knowledge are vital to my recovery. Day by day I learn to know and trust myself. The self-knowledge I gain in recovery is a tool I use to affirm myself, my values and my ideals.

I seek support from others, use daily readings, and other available opportunities to further my development. When I can, I remember to also draw on my culture, family, and community for the ways they are able to be supportive.

Feelings

Being happy is not the only happiness.
—Alice Walker, Songless

I have options for how I live, for how I feel, for my behavior. Today I am willing to look at possibilities and choices. As I take inventory of myself, I will find there are infinite possibilities and choices.

I can be happy with joy, or happy to know I can survive pain. I can be happy alone; happy with other people; happy with those who are different or similar to me. Allowing myself to experience the diversity of my feelings frees me to further explore and discover my identity and my true self in recovery.

Overcoming Obstacles

Forgiveness of both ourselves and others is said to be crucial for removing fear, anger and all the other obstacles that distort our relationships and prevent us from experiencing peace in them.

—*Foundation for Inner Peace*, A Course in Miracles

Forgiving others cleans out the pockets of despair and resentment that have tainted my actions for too long. Anger, fear and jealousy are potential barriers to sound relationships. If I have put up obstacles to honest relationships, I may need help tearing them down. Help comes in the form of forgiveness.

Forgiving myself clears my energy and strengthens my resolve to relate to others from a position of honesty and love. With the power of forgiveness, the obstacles that once interfered with honest and giving relationships disintegrate.

True Knowledge

Free every Monday through Friday—knowledge. Bring your own containers.
> *—graffiti at a high school in Dallas, Texas*

The good that flows through the universe is constant and is here for all. This source of light is not bound by tradition, judgment, fear, time or space. It is true knowledge such as this that relieves the weary traveler.

True knowledge expands me and brings me to a deeper understanding of my path to recovery. Sometimes the things I judge most harshly in others are the things I judge most harshly in myself. When I forgive myself, I can forgive others with greater ease.

Simplicity

I shut my eyes in order to see.
—Paul Gauguin

I used to think that the more scholarship, study and insight I could bring to my program, the better I would make it. Everything had to be compared to what I had learned from my family, from my culture, or from my community.

The only problem was that I wasn't getting any better. Then I remembered the wonderful old expression, "keep it simple." I realized my ego had been busy "easing God out." I had been so preoccupied with analyzing my program for living, I had not had any time to live it!

Purpose

I don't wish not to be a woman, but I'd certainly like to be a woman whose sense of purpose comes from within.
    —*Uno Chiyo,* Moho no Tensai (A Genius of Imitation)

Looking within myself, I will accept wisdom and choose what is best for me today. Willingness and openness to change is principal to my recovery. I can accept change as a positive adventure, even when the process presents difficulties or conflict within myself, my community, or with my family or friends.

As I discover the individuality of my purpose, I realize I deserve to be accepted by my community, even when I step outside cultural traditions. I will trust myself as I explore and find my own paths in life. Seeking my own sense of purpose draws from a courage I am grateful to have.

Animals

Acting "As If"

A problem is a chance for you to do your best.
—Duke Ellington

The other day I was watching some children ice skating. I noticed the older children were, for the most part, gliding around the ice. The younger children spent a lot of time just watching. Clearly they were thinking about how to skate, noting how it is done, and dreaming of the day when they could be so at ease on the ice. Just how do you keep your balance atop a metal blade on a slippery surface?

Not just by thinking. These little skaters might turn into accomplished ones by acting as if they know how to skate. In the same way, one of the lessons in my recovery is to try out new ways of living and behaving before I am completely assured of their outcome. I will remember the saying, "I am responsible for the effort, not the outcome."

Change

*The old woman I shall become will be quite
different from the woman I am now. Another
I is beginning ...*
—George Sand, Isadora

Choosing recovery is a gut-level change. It is
neither an intellectual choice nor one to make
somebody else happy. Recovery comes from the
core of my being, and my continued healing
depends on staying true to that core. There are
things I can do to support my growth, such as
reading and believing affirmations which remind
me to trust myself.

Acting 'as if' helps me through difficult times.
I can also speak from my heart and be authentic
in my relationships with others. These actions,
coupled with my willingness to continue my
recovery, open my heart to enduring change.

Keepers of Wisdom

The test of a people is how it behaves toward the old. It is easy to love children. Even tyrants and dictators make a point of being fond of children. But the affection and care for the old, the incurable, the helpless, are the true goldmines of a culture.
—Abraham Heschel

The elders in our communities can teach us to honor and respect the knowledge of our ancestors. Traditional teachings of many cultures revere the elderly of a community as keepers of wisdom, and it is an enduring truth that they are our best and closest link to culture and heritage. Today I will follow those teachings which are appropriate in my life.

Inner Voices

May you acknowledge
the voice within
And harken to its
power and wisdom.
        —*Mary Summer Rain,* Spirit Song

My inner wisdom comes from my spirit and my Source of Peace. This wisdom can be my energy source if I acknowledge it and trust in it. I can do this by affirming my self-worth, by valuing my choices, and by coming to know inner wisdom.

Although wisdom may speak softly, its messages can be clear and consistent. It is up to me to give it a voice. I will listen to my heart and then take the action I know is best for me.

Personal Awareness

"All right," said Quill, "start walking, and remember, don't try to walk with your head. Walk with your heart and you'll get through this darkness a lot easier."
—*Tony Shearer,* The Praying Flute

My unlimited potential as a human being is presented to me through the clarity I find in recovery. I try to keep my expectations realistic. It may be difficult to let go of familiar ideas or feelings, but recovery asks me to let go.

I unfold myself from illusions acquired from past experiences. The ability to see beyond misconceptions gives me courage and a freedom I had not known. With the understanding and patience found in my recovery, I can take small steps, which in turn help me to take bigger steps to heal and learn.

Self-Respect

If you want to be respected, you must respect yourself.
—*Spanish proverb*

Today I will give my self-respect room in which to grow. Earning respect begins with self-respect. I know if I constantly judge and criticize, self-esteem diminishes.

My self-image is visible to others, and is reflected in what comes back to me from others. When I love and accept who I am, flaws and all, my inner critic atrophies, and self-respect has room to grow.

Dance

life

Let's Dance

When you dance, the whole universe dances.
   —Jalaluddin Rumi

When everything seems impossible, and I have tried and tried, I can break through my frustrations with dance. Circles of grace, leaps of joy...they take me back into the world of the possible. Dancing unites my mind and body. I imagine my aura a hue of crimson and gold. Energy lifts me off the ground and blends me into the universal mind. Completely present in the moment, I am whole.

Movement transcends rational thought and superficial barriers—I do not need a special time or place. Alone or with someone else, at home or in the park, when I want to or when I need to, I can dance. Dancing allows me to play once again.

Alive

....how we live / is important business
latin night only monday
is contagious / dangerous
let us be ourselves / every day.
          —*Ntozake Shange,* "latin night is
monday"

When I center myself, I pull my physical energy into the warm core of my being. I am safe. I am whole. I can drop my reserve and let my vulnerability drift without restraint.

The shape of my body shifts and I become formless and complete. As I go deeper, my energy shimmers. I glow, I am alive, I am at peace. Anything is possible today if I believe.

Dance

Dreams

Your world is as big as you make it.
I know, for I used to abide
In the narrowest nest in a corner,
My wings pressing close to my side.
        —*Georgia Douglas Johnson,* "Your
World"

Part of my recovery is summoning the courage to hope and believe in my visions and goals. My vision and dreams come from my true self, which reflects my beliefs and hopes.

I will preserve my dreams in the face of conflict, injustice, or other adversity. I can use the tools of my recovery to respond to difficulties with honesty and self-respect, remaining true to my beliefs and my dreams. Today I will dare to remember my dreams in the dawn of a new day, and to look at both the questions and the answers they may provide.

Spiritual Center

There is no hidden poet in me, just a little piece of God that might grow into poetry.
*   —Etty Hillesum,* An Interrupted Life

My recovery can allow me to contact a spiritual center where there is peace and a state of knowing. Here I will transcend concepts that limit me. When I touch the realm of spiritual light, I live in a higher state of consciousness.

Trusting my inner source means I will find myself more caring, more willing to forgive, and more creative.

Believing in Life

Believe in life! Always human beings will live and progress to greater, broader and fuller life.
— *W.E.B. DuBois*

I believe in the process of life and in my process of recovery. To live fully means exploring and facing my fears, my joys, my past. To live fully means to be open to love and growth, anger and sorrow. This is the adventure of living—to discover and accept the wide range of my feelings.

The reflections of my recovery program also suggest that there are a variety of ways to believe in a Higher Power. Believing in life means that I can find my own beliefs and my own relationship to my Source of Peace.

Self-Image

We're like a tree that's planted by the water.
We shall not be moved!
        —from the spiritual "We Shall Not Be
Moved"

As I grow and evolve, a new self-image may
emerge also. I will remember to measure myself
by only my standards of inner or outer beauty.
The self-image I acquire in recovery is a salute to
my identity as I define myself.

Part of my uniqueness and individuality
comes from my cultural upbringing. Today I will
gratefully acknowledge my personal history and
my ancestral legacy. Recovery means that life
expands as I blend parts of myself, integrating my
past with my present.

Breath

A trifling matter, and fussy of me, but we all have our little ways.
   —Eeyore to Pooh, The House At Pooh Corner, *by A.A.Milne*

To hear my inner voices and to know my own truth, it is important to breathe. The answers I seek come from within me, from my core. Although I can learn from the experience, strength and hope of others, I seek also to trust my own heart. One way to know and speak truth is to close my eyes and to use my breath, the breath of life.

I let my breathing travel through all of me, giving light and life. I breathe to my core, to release any blocks, as the energy of my own truth flows. During moments such as this, I discover new realms of my own spirituality.

Source of Joy

I weep a lot. I thank God I laugh a lot too. The main thing in one's own private world is to try to laugh as much as you cry.
—Maya Angelou

Laughing through tears. I do it often. Laughter heals my heart when another tear would be more than I could stand. Laughter opens the door for light and energy to reach my soul. Acknowledging absurdities teaches me tolerance and love for others.

Laughter is both an expression and a source of joy. When I laugh, I end up more delighted than I was when I started. Laughter shared with friends is sacred. It is a moment of completion, of lives fully lived. Today I am primed for laughter.

Awe

People travel to wonder at the height of the mountains ...at the vast compass of the ocean, at the circular motion of the stars; they pass by themselves without wondering.
—St. Augustine

I stand in awe of nature. Whether I consider the delicate markings of a Siberian tiger or a field of mountain sage wet with dew, there is a sense of perfection in nature. Faced with my own frailties as a person, I may sometimes forget humankind is also part of nature. I may forget to notice the miracle of the human body, or to listen to my instincts.

Nurturing my connection to the natural world will open me to another dimension of myself. It will give me a better understanding and acceptance of others, and teach me there are many ways to live in our world. By respecting and deeply feeling my connection to all of life, I can affirm my identity.

161

Self-Acceptance

Nobody can be exactly like me. Sometimes even I have trouble doing it.
—Tallulah Bankhead

My path in recovery is to integrate all parts of me, to cherish myself and become whole. My history and experiences reveal both pain and pride. I can accept both as I savor the traditions of my culture.

Life expands as I explore and blend parts of myself. The self-acceptance I seek and acquire in recovery is a salute to my identity. I gratefully acknowledge my ancestral history and my personal past. I celebrate myself as a person.

Connection to the World Around Me

I danced in the morning when the world was
* begun*
And I danced in the moon and the stars and
* the sun.*
   —*hymn,* "Lord of the Dance," *by Sydney*
Carter

Forgiving myself and others reminds me that I am connected to the world, a part of a meaningful and vital culture. While I sometimes work alone with myself in recovery, these are also moments of affinity with the world around me.

My connection with the universe is a gift of my culture. I savor the contributions of my ancestry and carry them with me on my personal path.

Harmony

Happiness, rage, grief, delight...being moved by these passions each in due degree constitutes harmony.
　　　—*Alice Notley,* "Songs for the Unborn Second Baby"

Living passionately cannot be done without accepting risks, and opening myself up to the joys and opportunities offered in life makes me vulnerable to pain.

To avoid all pain would mean giving up love as well, and that sacrifice brings its own form of pain. Today I give thanks for all of life. The harmony of life is made up of both love and pain.

For the Common Good

As for myself, I have seen too much in my life to stand by and watch. It may not be in our power to evade our own suffering, but it is within our power to give our suffering some meaning. And it is in combating the suffering of others that we find meaning in our own.
—Elie Wiesel

The "ostrich syndrome" is powerful. There are times I just want to put my head in the sand to avoid the suffering in the world. But life is not lived in a vacuum. Inner strength comes from my connection to all of life.

I am a part of the whole. Although I am not responsible for the actions of others, I am affected by them. Today I will acknowledge my connection to all of life. I will treat others with compassion and dignity, and look for ways to help those in need.

Spirit Source

Breathe gently, naturally, with gratitude.
Breathe...relax your body...rest...and as you
do this become aware that inside you there is
a healing spirit, the resilient radiance of your
birthright.
  —*Alla Renée Bozarth,* Journey through
Grief

  The breath of life is both powerful and
gentle. When I am anxious or angry, I can calm
myself by taking deep, slow breaths. I can follow
the air flowing in and out of my body. As it goes
to my center, I envision my spirit receiving the
breath of life.

  I am revived, my strength renewed. As my
breath is released, it carries out tension which
may have entrapped my spirit. Freed, my spirit
flows through my arms, my fingers, down to
every toe. My heart is opened, and I am centered.

Dance
========

A New Order

*The way you use the word "God" does not show
whom you mean—but, rather, what you mean.*
—Ludwig Wittgenstein

I await the day when the sacredness of all life
is honored. I look to the day when people of all
races live in peace with each other, when cultural
differences are treasured as a source of creativity
and compassion.

I look to a day when the energy spent on
destruction is finally turned to creating mental
and physical well-being. Until then, I will demonstrate these values, hopes and dreams by living
a life that is true to my ideals, my world, and my
Creator. I can have peace in my heart, peace in
my world.

Pure Heart

May your mind forever
sparkle like a star.
Your heart remain
pure as new fallen snow,
And your spirit forever
sense the wonderment
of a child.
　　　　　—*Mary Summer Rain,* Spirit Song

Today I stand in awe of the beauty in the world. I am filled with wonder at the miracles I see around me, and my heart opens to the joy of living. I give thanks for the love I receive and for that which I give.

Dance

Free of Judgment

Each of us has a song in our heart. Through thought, through action, each one is creating vibration in the atmosphere.

—Dhyani Ywahoo, Voices of Our Ancestors

I smile when feeling the resonance of life. I can start the chain reaction today by relating to others free of presumptions and judgments. To generate respect and goodwill, I can center myself in love and faith, reminding myself of my own worthiness.

The wonderful side effect of being open to the goodness in others is reinforcement of my own joy. It becomes an ever-expanding and self-perpetuating circle. Imagine a world where everyone reveres life.

Self-Responsibility

Let us not be blind to our differences, but let us also direct attention to our common interests...we can help make the world safe for diversity.
—John Fitzgerald Kennedy

I am in charge of my life today. So many of us have parts of our past that are hurtful or unpleasant. Whether standing in the midst of past memories or in the face of tribulation today, I can choose to believe in myself and in the fullest possibilities of life.

My voice is an important one, and I can use it in being responsible for myself. Rather than escape from these experiences and memories, today I can create my life to be as I want. Each time I take responsibility for myself and am true to myself, I validate who I am. My recovery and my identity are strengthened.

Dance

The Best I Can Do

Dear God,
I am doing the best I can.
    —Children's Letters to God, *compiled*
by Stuart Hample and Eric Marshall

The best I can do is enough. When I am feeling judged by others—or when I am passing judgment—I can stop, examine my thoughts, and ask myself what the basis for judgment is.

Am I trying to meet someone else's expectations, or a vision that does not match up with mine? The best I can do I all that I can do.

Waiting

Starting all over, it's kind of difficult saying where you want to go. You go step by step, waiting and waiting, and, I guess, being a sprinter, its hard to wait.
—*Wyomia Tyus*

Impatient for change, I push and struggle against my own resistance and doubt. But sometimes the more I push, the more I strengthen my resistance and block the flow of my being. Recovery is a process, and sometimes it is a process that does not go according to my plans.

I can trust that I am experiencing what is best for me at the pace that is best for me. This may release my anxiety and lighten my load. I can acknowledge when I am confused or impatient, and trust that my vision will clear.

⌘

Dance

Love Lines

For one human being to love another human being: that is perhaps the most difficult task that has been entrusted to us, the ultimate task, the final test and proof, the work for which all other work is merely preparation.
—*Rainer Maria Rilke*

In advertising, love is often treated like a commodity. The message is that all we have to do is buy a product being advertised and we will get love. Of course, real life is different. Abiding love is not to be bartered or bought. When love comes with strings attached, it is conditional—transformed and weakened.

I can package the love I give with "love lines"—lines which will keep communication open, lines which will connect me to my loved ones without judgment, lines which allow a two-way path of respect and trust.

Garden of Dreams

I have wrapped my dreams in a silken cloth,
And laid them away in a box of gold
  —*Countee Cullen,* "For a Poet"

I nurture my garden of dreams, tending to it with love and compassion. I receive comfort and guidance from my dreams. When I doubt the world's goodness or my ability to change, I can be still and give my dreams room to grow.

I can use deep breathing and other relaxation techniques to quiet my critical thoughts, to banish the "yes, buts," the "if onlys" and the "I can'ts." With my critic turned off, my garden of dreams becomes a vivid field of possibilities.

Affirming Myself

Lift every voice and sing
Till earth and heaven ring,
Ring with the harmonies of Liberty
        —*James Weldon Johnson,* "Lift Every
Voice and Sing"

My recovery reflects the belief I have in myself—that I belong in the world as I am today. I affirm myself through self-discovery and discovery of my Source of Peace.

If I have lost connections to my culture, my heritage, my true inner self, or my Source of Peace, I now choose to discover and explore ways to reclaim myself.

Shadow Dance

Feeling light within, I walk.
  —Navajo night chant

I dance in the moonlight to celebrate my life.
My feet skip over the Mother ground. My shadow
skims the surface of her rivers. With my spirit
reverberating among the stars, I offer up gratitude and sheer joy.

I honor and revel in my changes. My journey
will continue, but in this moment it is complete.
I am perfect. I am whole.

New Shades of Meaning

This we know. All things are connected like the blood which unites one family. All things are connected.
—*Chief Seattle*

Part of my foundation in recovery is to understand being powerless over other people, places and situations. Recovery is like an ascending spiral staircase, building on the wisdom gained in climbing the step below. There are no certificates of graduation saying we are no longer powerless over our addiction.

I try to keep clear in my mind the difference between a spiritual sense of powerlessness and the type which means persecution or oppression. It can be a relief to know that I am powerless in the more spiritual sense, and to know I can ask for help. In my powerlessness, I float like a feather, brushing the face of God. Being powerless, I am free.

_____

Clear Feelings

What we call "I" is just a swinging door which moves when we inhale and when we exhale.
—*Shunryu Suzuki,* Zen Mind, Beginner's Mind

Self-honesty is part of my path of freedom to discover myself. I can identify my strengths and shortcomings, and remember that neither define me. My recovery gives me clarity to experience all my feelings as I begin to know myself. This fullness enhances my courage and confidence, and my feelings enrich life as I choose a path of improvement.

Dance

Opportunities to Learn

True worth is in being, not seeming—
In doing, each day that goes by,
Some little good—
—Alice Cary, "Nobility"

As I try to change harmful patterns in my life, I can move into new territory. In my recovery I will attempt ways of being that are new to me, and sometimes I will make mistakes. This is to be expected, because I am human.

Still, at times I may find myself fearful of making a mistake. When I take on the challenge of improving myself, however, I will continue to grow and heal, even if I do make a mistake. Today I will remember that mistakes are opportunities to learn.

Small Steps

You have brains in your head. You have feet in your shoes. You can steer yourself in any direction you choose.
    —*Theodore Seuss Geisell (Dr. Seuss),*
Oh, The Places You'll Go

Today I truly am committed to taking action to change and grow. If I wait for the perfect time or opportunity to go after my dreams, I risk never realizing them at all. The more I put off taking first steps, waiting for the "right" moment, the larger that first step grows in my mind.

I can start by taking small steps and acknowledging my day's successes. With each step, I will reaffirm belief in myself, and my vision will become clearer and stronger. With each step, I will participate more fully in my life.

Fire
renewal

Rebuilding

That sorrow, tears and evil, all are good;
We know it matters not what we have been
But this and always this: what we shall be.
　　　　—*Angelina Weld Grimké,* "Then and
Now"

In the midst of a concern or a painful situation, it is difficult to see what may come from it. At first, pain is swift and terrible, leaving a gaping wound. In fact, it is hard to even want to see the potential. Yet pain and difficulty can lead to important life lessons.

When grief breaks my heart, it also breaks down the walls I have built to protect myself. But as I heal, I have a choice. Rather than rebuild walls, making them even thicker, I can leave myself open to love.

Sweet Forgiveness

Never does the human soul appear so strong as when it forgoes revenge, and dares forgive an injury.
—*E. H. Chapin*

Forgiving those who have done me harm sweetens my life; it is a deed that I do for me, not for the person who hurt me. If a hurt is great, it may take some time before I can see my way clear to forgiveness.

It can be much easier to forgive someone who unintentionally hurts my feelings than it is to forgive someone who deliberately goes out of his or her way to do me harm. When I forgive, I am taking a big step toward empowerment.

Beauty

*The largest grief will paint itself into the longest
beauty.*
—*Gloria Frym,* "Strange Fruit"

The human spirit has a tremendous ability to
meet hardship with compassion and courage.
Even in the most tragic of circumstances, people
can face fear and grief, and find love. It is not
unusual to hear of personal transformation coming out of someone's life-threatening experience.
There is suddenly no more time or energy for old
defenses and misconceptions.

When we confront our mortality, we realize
it is time to forgive. But I do not want to wait until
life circumstances force me to choose love. I can
choose to forgive myself and others today. I can
choose love now.

Heal Through Pain

I have reached a point in my life where I understand the pain and the challenges, and my attitude is one of standing up with open arms to meet them all.
—*Myrlie Evers*

When I feel pain, be it physical or emotional, I can choose to ignore it, or I can embrace it. If I acknowledge the pain, I can gain perspective. Eventually I will be able to locate its source. Then I have the opportunity for deep healing.

Fire

Restoring Justice Within

In the darkest hour the soul is replenished and given strength to continue and endure.
—Heart Warrior Chosa

When I feel isolated or unjustly treated, I can restore justice within myself by adhering to my personal sense of integrity. I remember I can change only my own behavior, and no one else's.

If an outside element interferes with my dreams and hopes, I can still strongly hold my belief in those dreams. My hopes and aspirations are a vital part of my recovery.

renewal

Personal Power

Our right is to live and be free;
Freedom will not come from outside.
It is only in ourselves united.
　　　　—fisher's song, Philippines

I can find joy and harmony by being at one
with my spirituality. When sitting in silence I can
feel life's energy, and sense the true knowledge
that comes not only from my intellectual understanding, but also from the spiritual guidance I
find within me.

In realizing my uniqueness, I can begin to
drop the erroneous notions of my being which I
may have received from others. By dropping
those notions, I regain my personal power in
recovery. I can begin to gently let go of false
concepts of myself as I discover my personal
power.

Fire

Journey to the Soul

Look within, and seek That.
—Jalaluddin Rumi

Recovery is a journey to my essence—my soul. It is the core that houses my love, my feelings of worthiness, my creativity. Love and imagination feed my soul, which in turn nourishes my healing. As I think of caring for my soul, of giving my essence just what it needs, my faith flourishes, a constant reminder of the promise of life.

Each decision reflects my search for deeper meaning in life. My soul seeks ways of being which validate my existence, that are manifestations of my ideals and values. Today my choices will be guided by the best interests of my soul. By taking care of my soul, I take care of myself.

Regeneration

Whatever your past has been, you have a spotless future.
—*anonymous*

Hurtful or unpleasant memories from the past have only as much power as I give them. Today I can let go of these memories, loosening their hold on me, and letting them dissolve.

This release opens my heart, and fills me with hope and excitement as I joyously begin to create the life I want. I can embrace the present, trusting my faith and my wisdom to guide and empower me. I will open myself to faith.

When I Can Laugh

The importance of humor should never be forgotten. For sense of humor changes the quality and character of our entire cultural life.

—*Lin Yutang*

Sometimes I have to laugh, even though I know recovery is serious. My efforts to change how I am living my life are not to be taken lightly—they take energy, focus, commitment, and courage.

But humor is also a necessary ingredient. When I can laugh at myself and at the absurdities which abound in this world, I am able to take the edge off of my frustrations. My impatience may evaporate, and I regain my perspective, which makes it easier to get back to my basic values and desires.

Secrets

*All sorrows can be borne if you put them into a
story or tell a story about them.*
—Isak Dinesen

At a meeting the other night I found myself
getting more and more upset with the speaker,
because this person was up there saying all those
things that caused me pain, but were too difficult
and painful for me to say myself.

I realized, gratefully, that my Higher Power
had given me this speaker to demonstrate that
what I was afraid to say was speakable. I learned
that someone somewhere has lived at least one
experience similar to mine, teaching me to step
out of the isolation of feeling terminally unique.

Fire

Shyness

Now that it comes to answering your questions and telling you about myself, I feel oddly shy. Not that this is a reason to hold back; in fact, I deem it a sign to press on.
—*Nick Bantock*, Griffin & Sabine

Young children are often shy around strangers. This is part of their exploration of the world; they experience new things tentatively at first, and then with more confidence. In my recovery, I have periods of shyness too. I am exploring new ways of being, new ways of seeing. Sometimes I am tentative in my actions, and shy about announcing my discoveries to the world.

While I may not yet be confident about my transformation, putting my thoughts into words can help me clarify what is happening to me. I can try to explain them aloud to a friend or family member who will listen without judging, or I can write my feelings and thoughts. Putting changes into words brings them into sharp focus.

Cloak of Colors

They say you should not suffer through the past. You should be able to wear it like a loose garment, take it off, and let it drop.
—*Eva Jessye*

I like to think of my past as a cloak of many colors. I carry it with me always, but I only wear it when I need to. Some days I need the ancient earth tones of my ancestors to give me comfort and protect me from the elements. Other days, to keep me moving forward, I wear the brilliant golds and reds of my recent changes.

Sometimes I forget I am wrapped in my past, until I realize that I am being dragged down by extra weight. Then I stop and take off my cloak. My past is part of me. How I wear it is up to me.

Fire

Truth Will Set Me Free

Those who, in all humility,
Listen to the Truth
Praise it and faithfully follow it,
Will be endowed with innumerable merits.
        —*Abbot Zenkei Shibayama,* A Flower
Does Not Talk

When I am confused about a situation, I can
pause and try to listen for the truth. Being aware
of the gray layers that can veil the truth helps me
recognize the core.

I know I can trust my instincts. Like a muscle
developed by exercise, my inner alarm is honed
by using truth as a guide. If I approach life by
seeking its truthful essence, I can eventually
decide upon the best choices for me.

Living My Changes

Tell me and I'll forget. Show me and I may not remember. Involve me and I'll understand.
—*Native American saying*

My journey moves forward only when I incorporate healing actions into my day to day existence.

I can read inspirational stories of self-discovery and healing. I can watch my friends learning to integrate their cultures and ancestries into their daily lives. I can give money to support others' actions for peace and justice. All of these actions support and affirm my own recovery, but to further my healing I must live my changes. Today I will take charge of my healing by turning my beliefs into actions.

Fire

Transformation

The most dangerous of our prejudices reign in ourselves against ourselves. To dissolve them is a creative act.

—*Hugo Von Hofmannsthal,* The Book of Friends

My transformation is a lifelong process. I continue to recreate myself to better fit my ideals and dreams. Part of this regeneration means addressing my prejudices, and dislodging them is no simple chore.

Prejudice is like a vapor that can permeate every crack and crevice of a surface. In the vitality of my recovery, I no longer limit myself to what I have been or how I am perceived. I am busy creating who I am.

A Day at a Time

In knowing how to overcome little things, a centimeter at a time, gradually when bigger things come, you're prepared. You're not taken by surprise, you're not even angry or upset. It just arouses your spirit to do more.
—Katherine Dunham

Disappointment may bring up sludge from the past. But if I remember that my feelings are affected by the past, it is easier to keep current disappointments in perspective. I can then move on, keeping in mind that healing is lifelong.

Today I will remember that my recovery is made up of a series of small steps. I always have the opportunity to try again. And each time I try and succeed, I am in better shape to take the next step.

Fire

In the Moment

First keep the peace within yourself, then you can also bring peace to others.
—*Thomas à Kempis*

There came a point in my life when I made a decision to explore spirituality further, calling on the Author of Peace to help me work at living in the present. Now I can allow my emotions to flow more easily.

If some past situations are not resolved, I will do what it takes so that the past does not interferc with the present. Today I can unclog the past not yet resolved, as I release old emotions and find new room for the present. Each day is an opportunity to resolve challenges as they appear in my life.

Opportunity

Oh, warm is the waiting for joys, my dears!
And it cannot be too long.

> —*Gwendolyn Brooks,* "A Streete in
Bronzeville"

In my recovery I respect the process of time
and its passage. Each moment I can live with as
much fullness as I wish, expressing the best of my
desires and abilities. The present is an opportunity to discover and expand.

The emotional strength I find through my
explorations teaches me to learn about and
understand the role my roots play in recovery.
Today I can accept my life as a blend of numerous
and varied influences, to be lived day by day.

Fire

Healing in Forgiveness

Forgiveness is not an occasional act, it is a permanent attitude.
  —*Martin Luther King*

I am participating in a lifelong transformation, and learning to forgive is a part of my evolution. Forgiving can remove lingering feelings of being victimized, although I may need to ponder the anger and resentment I feel before I can be forgiving. There may be steps I need to take to resolve these feelings—perhaps even legal steps. Forgiveness does not mean foregoing justice.

Still, eventual forgiveness is important to my healing, as is knowing the joys of life. To enhance my growth, I will also try to make room for joy and laughter.

Spiritual Tolerance

*Oh God who is called a thousand names, and
so graciously answers to them all.*
   —anonymous

We must be free to pray, meditate and
contemplate life in our diverse ways. Prayer is
part of my way of living day to day, and in my
prayers, I pray for freedom, for myself and for
others.

I can go to sleep each night with a cleaner
slate when I make sure that respect for the
beliefs of others has touched my day.

ﷺ

Fire

The Awakened Mind

May the clear light of awakened mind become apparent. May each person sing an affirmation of the inherent beauty. May the mind that unites all beings be recognized as the foundation of our shared existence in the family of humanity.

—*Dhyani Ywahoo,* Voices of Our Ancestors

Awakened to the wonder of life, I can now see beauty and hear the love that surrounds me. Harmful behavior or self-destructive acts that once may have clouded my vision have dropped away, putting the possibilities of life in clear focus.

My mind races with the colors of new dreams. The complexity of existence excites me, and its richness and depth promise ever-expanding joy. Like a child, I delight in the amazement of everyday life. The warmth of the sun protects me. The rain tickles me. I have awakened to life.

renewal

Recovering from Slips

Bear with me. I'll get back on track. Actually I'm not off the track. I'm off the train, but not off the track.
—*Ruth Beebe Hill*

On my path of recovery, I accept that slipping is not the same as failing. In the past, "failing" was a word heavily weighted by expectations.

Now I understand that making a mistake or having a setback is just that—a misstep. It does not necessarily change the direction in which I am moving. Today I will examine my recent past for missteps. I will look at situations honestly, forgive myself for mistakes, and then get back on my path of recovery.

Fire

Renewing Energy

Love is the most durable power in the world.
—Martin Luther King, Jr.

Love is the greatest renewable energy source in the world. The more that love is given, the more there is to give. I can tap this energy source by loving myself unconditionally, and letting self-love become an internal everlasting flame which keeps my faith alive. This flame kindles my dreams and powers belief in myself.

The power of love envelops me, and guides my way in the world. My energy source becomes even stronger when I can give love to others unconditionally. When someone is given unconditional love, it sparks love in return. Today I will be conscious of the power of love within me. I will draw strength from the flame and share it willingly.

Creating Personal Truth

You never find yourself until you face the truth.
—*Pearl Bailey*

I am the consciousness that creates my reality. No matter what the state of affairs in the world at large, the tools of recovery give me a personal power to create a new, more positive inner reality.

I am the thinker of my own thoughts and I have a choice of what I believe. By following my inner light, I can move beyond the fears of yesterday, and reflections about tomorrow will comfort me.

Fire

Lifelong Transformation

A single event can awaken within us a stranger totally unknown to us. To live is to be slowly born.
—Antoine de Saint-Exupéry

In my recovery I have learned to open myself to more than one path. Although I set my direction, I welcome opportunities and surprises that I am sure to meet along the way.

Sometimes the surprises are wake-up calls. I might realize that I am slipping into an old pattern, or I may meet an aspect of myself that is difficult to encounter.

Life is full of possibilities, and I can choose those which teach me new ways of being. With each new choice, another part of me unfolds.

renewal

Try Something New

It's never too late—in fiction or in life—to revise.
—Nancy Thayer

Hostility and acts of rage are occurring throughout the world today. As an individual, I can only control my own actions and treat others with dignity and respect. I can choose to be compassionate and fair-minded in all my dealings with others.

I can choose to accept cultural differences among people as valuable to our shared existence on this planet. Today I choose to relate to the person rather than to the skin color, gender or class.

Blessings of The Soul

Prayer clarifies our hopes and intentions. It helps us discover our true aspirations, the pangs we ignore, the longings we forget. It is an act of self-purification, a quarantine for the soul. It gives us the opportunity to be honest, to say what we believe, and to stand for what we say.

—Abraham Heschel

Prayer is a pause to let God move me. I may choose to pray through song, drawing, writing or silent meditation. Whatever the method, it is a time when I quiet my rational thoughts and let my intuition lead me.

Through prayer, I unfold myself to receive the grace and tender touch of the Creator of Peace. I open myself to the beauty of the sacred, and let prayer heal my injuries and replenish my soul. When I pray, I am blessed by the power which has created all we know. I am renewed and comforted.

renewal

A Quiet Place

...so come with me to this place
i know where music expects me
& when she finds me
i am bathed in the ocean's breath
& left with the soft glory of my laughter
   —Ntozake Shange, "Nappy Edges"

Within each of us is a quiet place that sprouts serenity and joy. As we draw from our authentic selves, we restore abilities to laugh and express joy. In recovery, I will delight in discovering my own true joys as I learn the importance of understanding and accepting my feelings.

I can let laughter into my life, and when appropriate, it can help in overcoming adversity. There is humor, as well as challenge, in living and working in our diverse society. Laughter can renew me, provide comfort, and aid both emotional and physical healing.